Managing Information in Higher Education

E. Michael Staman, *Editor*

NEW DIRECTIONS FOR INSTITUTIONAL RESEARCH

PATRICK T. TERENZINI, *Editor-in-Chief*
University of Georgia

MARVIN W. PETERSON, *Associate Editor*
University of Michigan

Number 55, Fall 1987

Paperback sourcebooks in
The Jossey-Bass Higher Education Series

Jossey-Bass Inc., Publishers
San Francisco • London

E. Michael Staman (ed.).
Managing Information in Higher Education.
New Directions for Institutional Research, no. 55.
Volume XIV, Number 3.
San Francisco: Jossey-Bass, 1987.

New Directions for Institutional Research
Patrick T. Terenzini, *Editor-in-Chief*
Marvin W. Peterson, *Associate Editor*

New Directions for Institutional Research is published quarterly by
Jossey-Bass Inc., Publishers (publication number USPS 098-830), and is
sponsored by the Association for Institutional Research. The volume
and issue numbers above are included for the convenience of libraries.
Second-class postage paid at San Francisco, California, and at
additional mailing offices. POSTMASTER: Send address changes to
Jossey-Bass Inc., Publishers, 433 California Street, San Francisco,
California 94104.

Editorial correspondence should be sent to the Editor-in-Chief,
Patrick T. Terenzini, Institute of Higher Education, University of
Georgia, Athens, Georgia 30602.

Library of Congress Catalog Card Number LC 85-645339

International Standard Serial Number ISSN 0271-0579

International Standard Book Number ISBN 1-55542-947-5

Cover art by WILLI BAUM

Manufactured in the United States of America

Ordering Information

The paperback sourcebooks listed below are published quarterly and can be ordered either by subscription or single copy.

Subscriptions cost $48.00 per year for institutions, agencies, and libraries. Individuals can subscribe at the special rate of $36.00 per year *if payment is by personal check*. (Note that the full rate of $48.00 applies if payment is by institutional check, even if the subscription is designated for an individual.) Standing orders are accepted.

Single copies are available at $11.95 when payment accompanies order. (California, New Jersey, New York, and Washington, D.C., residents please include appropriate sales tax.) For billed orders, cost per copy is $11.95 plus postage and handling.

Substantial discounts are offered to organizations and individuals wishing to purchase bulk quantities of Jossey-Bass sourcebooks. Please inquire.

Please note that these prices are for the academic year 1987–88 and are subject to change without notice. Also, some titles may be out of print and therefore not available for sale.

To ensure correct and prompt delivery, all orders must give either the *name of an individual* or an *official purchase order number*. Please submit your order as follows:

Subscriptions: specify series and year subscription is to begin.
Single Copies: specify sourcebook code (such as, IR1) and first two words of title.

Mail orders for United States and Possessions, Latin America, Canada, Japan, Australia, and New Zealand to:
Jossey-Bass Inc., Publishers
433 California Street
San Francisco, California 94104

Mail orders for all other parts of the world to:
Jossey-Bass Limited
28 Banner Street
London EC1Y 8QE

New Directions for Institutional Research Series
Patrick T. Terenzini *Editor-in-Chief*
Marvin W. Peterson, *Associate Editor*

88- 12.36

The Association for Institutional Research was created in 1966 to benefit, assist, and advance research leading to improved understanding, planning, and operation of institutions of higher education. Publication policy is set by its Publications Board.

For information about the Association for Institutional Research, write:

AIR Executive Office
314 Stone Building
Florida State University
Tallahassee, FL 32306

(904) 644-4470

Contents

Editor's Notes

In recent years higher education has begun the long and somewhat difficult process of changing the ways it collects, stores, retrieves, analyzes, and uses information. Colleges and universities are beginning to view management information and discipline content information as resources, and the management of those resources is the subject of this volume of *New Directions for Institutional Research*.

Centralized management information systems that exist solely to maintain data and support user requests for reports are becoming anachronisms. Terms such as "distributing data processing" (an activity that results in the placement of machine resources, and often personnel resources and operational responsibilities, in user offices) and "information centers" (organizational structures staffed with experts whose typical mission is to facilitate end-user computing through teaching, consulting, and often direct assistance) describe how centralized systems are being replaced. These changes are also spawning fundamental transformations in the conceptions of, and roles played by, institutional researchers and other data analysts, computing center administrators and staff, and even senior managers themselves.

The management of information depends, first and foremost, on good administrative and office systems. Of equal importance is an appropriately structured telecommunications system to manage the flow of voice, data, and video information throughout the institution. The management of information also includes a planned program to support research and instructional computing, areas in which change is even more rapid than in administrative support areas.

The first step, then, is to build a foundation. Only when this foundation is in place can a university begin to use distributed techniques and information centers to maximize the return on its investment in these resources. Only then does the institution have a base on which it can build a program to strategically manage and use its information resources.

Serious issues are raised by these new information processing environments, ranging from how to build and maintain a foundation for their existence to how to manage them for the optimal benefit of the institution. As academic and administrative units become increasingly involved in the collection, storage, retrieval, analysis, and use of data, and as they develop their own analytical and decision-support systems, questions of significant institutional, managerial, and financial consequence are raised.

If, for example, a college or university contemplates distributing its computing activities throughout the institution, questions immediately

1

arise: Which activities should be distributed; how much; what control; which levels of authority and budgetary responsibility; and what relationships must be maintained with the central facility? These questions, and others like them, have operational, managerial, and financial implications.

This sourcebook is aimed at developing an environment in which an information management strategy can evolve, and succeed. The volume begins with a chapter by E. Michael Staman that provides an overview of several alternative models for the delivery of computing services. These models have developed over the years, and so the chapter seeks to explore the relative fit of each model in today's computing and communications environment. Of particular importance are the questions surrounding the new systems integration imperative facing most colleges and universities today. This imperative results from the seemingly random growth of technological resources within our institutions. One excellent example of a problem contributing to the imperative is the increasingly frequent need to develop a summary of information located on a number of data files—often structured in incompatible architectures, resident on separate and incompatible computers, and stored on separate and incompatible networks.

Chapters on office systems, academic computing, and telecommunications follow the overview. Perhaps as significant as their content is the fact that just five years ago an information management sourcebook probably would not have contained such chapters. At best, mention of the material would have been in a future context.

Although there is a body of literature discussing the office environment, little has been written about office systems in the context of information resources management. Joan Day's chapter begins with the correct assumption that office environments are no longer separate and distinct components of college and university technological infractures. Office workers, aptly described as knowledge workers, have become technology users, hence computer users. Day's observation is central to her theme: "They [colleges and universities] are understanding that, while word processing, desktop publishing, personal computer-based spreadsheet and data base programs, electronic mail, local area networks, and other office technologies are specialized and targeted for the office end-user, these technologies are becoming increasingly integrated with such traditional technologies as voice communications and "back office" administrative computing systems.

Often called instructional and research computing, academic computing has clearly moved from central facilities to classrooms, faculty offices, and often faculty homes. Interestingly, many of the lessons learned during three decades of developing academic computing services are now being applied to the problems of distributing administrative computing services. Stanley Warren's chapter begins by tracing the development of academic computing from its infancy to the present, and provides several provocative suggestions about both its future and its impact on colleges and universities. According to Warren, the challenge is not in applying what we have learned so as to meet traditional goals of increased efficiency, but rather in applying technology to help us change the fundamental nature of our institutions, and possibly our educational processes.

The chapter on telecommunications, by Alan Creutz, analyzes the potential of communications for colleges and universities today. Through examples one can discover ways to enhance administrative, instructional, and research activities. In addition, one can find methods for exploring what are rapidly becoming known as mission critical applications for higher education—in this case the issue of student recruitment and retention. Creutz concludes his chapter with discussions on management, centralization, and planning for telecommunications.

If telecommunications is the glue that permits true systems integration, then it is the use of fourth-generation tools by end-users that is the catalyst for distributing newly available products and services throughout the information resources structure. Gregory Litaker's discussion of applications development environments clearly indicates that the traditional environment of the past has been expanded to include at least two new environments, the information specialist and end-user environments. In each environment there are significant differences in the nature of the users and their experience with both fourth-generation tools and the applications to which the tools will be directed. Litaker has included a case study to exemplify the concepts developed during the chapter.

What the first five chapters describe, then, is a new information resources environment. This environment has resulted in new roles and responsibilities for institutional research, especially in the areas of data administration and management. In their chapter on data administration, Richard McKinney, John Schott, Deborah Teeter, and Linda Mannering discuss how to deal with an ever-increasing number and variety of users who place prime importance on access to data. The chapter reviews several key issues relating to the decentralization of data, including data access, integrity, manipulation, analysis, interpretation, and reporting. The insights provided throughout the chapter are reenforced by a case study at the University of Kansas, Lawrence. The data administration function there was assigned to the University Office of Institutional Research and Planning, and the experiences of the Office to date are reported in the study.

The explosion of technology in the information age and the shift in managerial style as a response to demands for accountability have created a new and somewhat disruptive situation for those who translate data into information for use in decision making. This providing of facts consists of two steps: (1) summarizing data into information, and (2) focusing that information on a specific situation as useable knowledge. In their chapter on decision support in the information age, Gerald McLaughlin,

Josetta McLaughlin, and Richard Howard provide us with a better understanding of these two steps. The chapter effectively concludes this volume's chapters on foundation building and impact and makes a natural transition to the final chapter on policy.

One of the areas most often neglected is that of policy for the management and control of university data resources. This neglect has become especially worrisome as software and hardware architectures have advanced to the point where on line systems, data bases, and distributed computing have become increasingly common. E. Michael Staman's chapter on policy issues provides definitions and offers recommendations that administrators can employ as institutional policy. Most college and university data centers should be able to adopt the recommendations, rewriting and tailoring them to their specific environments.

The material in this volume of *New Directions for Institutional Research* has been organized to take the reader from foundations to delivery mechanisms, impacts, and policy issues. The volume describes many of the key elements in the development of an information management program, and the policies and procedures that must be in place if the program is to be successful and sustainable over time.

Managing information in higher education need not be a labyrinthine and uncertain adventure, although it also cannot be accomplished through standardized formulas, luck, or charismatic leadership. Team efforts, an eye toward systems integration, some formulas, some charisma, leadership, and a lot of hard work are all key ingredients. It is the intent of this sourcebook to promote the development of an environment in which an information management strategy can evolve, and succeed.

E. Michael Staman
Editor

E. Michael Staman has been involved in higher education since 1966, serving as a faculty member and in various administrative capacities in computing, institutional research, and planning.

*Wise selection from among alternative tools and models for
delivering computing services will maximize the return
on the investment that colleges and universities have
made in technology.*

Tools and Models
for Computing and
Communications Services

E. Michael Staman

The forces that currently affect university computing and information
processing executives have evolved significantly from those of thirty years
ago, when the key issues were capability, capacity, and compatibility.
Today's issues include such previously non-traditional activities as supporting information centers, deciding when and how to use "productivity
tools," dealing with purchasing rather than building new services, and
providing leadership in the overall area of integrating college- and univer-
sity-wide systems into one cohesive service.

    While computing executives, increasingly known as Chief Infor-
mation officers (CIOs), still have clear responsibility for central computing
services, the nature of those services is no longer the same as in years past.
Central computing's role as a provider of traditional computing systems
and services has been expanded to include activities ranging from network
planning and management to consulting with what is becoming a largely
self-directed community of users. The priorities for the future are almost
the inverse of those of ten, or even five years ago, with the role of systems
integrators rapidly evolving as the top priority:

    • Integrate a diverse set of systems, networks, and hardware

E. M. Staman (ed.). *Managing Information in Higher Education.*
New Directions for Institutional Research, no. 55. San Francisco: Jossey-Bass, Summer 1987.

- Act as information center and caretakers of data/information resources
- Offer network planning and management
- Provide standards and procedures
- Act as consultants or advisors to a largely self-directed community of users
- Set up new, specialized services
- Operate, provide, develop traditional systems and computing services.

The purpose of this chapter is to explore the various tools and models for providing computing services that have developed as a result of changing technologies and user abilities. The questions that the chapter considers are: What were the key ingredients of each model or tool at the time of its appearance? How and where does each model or tool fit into the spectrum of approaches to providing computing and communications services today? What is the nature of the new systems integration imperative?

The chapter begins with a review of the original model, "computing classic." It will also consider tools and models such as distributed computing, fourth-generation languages, information centers, and the use of the computing service industry, including "buy versus build" decisions. The conclusions should not come as a surprise to many—all of the models fit, and the systems-integration problems of today include all of the leadership and management problems that have arisen during the past thirty years. Capability, capacity, and compatibility are still issues, but the key issue turns out to be how to best fit the range of alternatives available into the solutions required by universities today.

Computing Classic

Older is not always better. An IBM 704, for example, cost about $2 million, had 32,000 words of memory, and cost $800 per month to power and cool. The mean time between failure was several days.

Central management was clearly the organizational structure for the classic model. A central pool of resources provided operations, systems development, and all other services. Development models were batch oriented, without data bases as we know them today, and with all of the problems associated with coding forms, centralized data entry, and difficult ad hoc reporting requirements. Providing support for modules of what should have been a system, but was really a sequence of programs designed by different people at different times, with different architectures and duplicate data structures, was an extremely difficult, if not impossible, task. Capability, capacity, and compatibility problems were the key issues. Users, and to some extent, data center executives, were not sure what was possible through the use of an electronic data processing (EDP) facility. Almost invariably, needs quickly exceeded storage capacity, memory capacity, and processor capacity. Nothing seemed compatible with anything else.

The classic model was used for many years, and is still an important alternative. Today, the model does not really exist in its purest form, since by definition the acquisition of even one microcomputer to perform processing at any non-central location starts the process, and problems, of distributing computing.

Universities should not, in fact cannot, do without the classic model. If they exist for no other purpose, central facilities will continue to support university-owned data bases and to support areas that cannot efficiently meet their own information processing requirements. The term "computing begets computing" clearly applies. The evolution of microcomputing and distributed computing has caused greater sophistication on the part of the user community, and as a natural consequence, greater pressure on central facilities.

Distributed Functions

At first, there was the question of whether or not to distribute. The issues were whether computing executives could maintain control, synchronization of data bases, and compatibility. Capacity was much less of a concern, since one could conceivably continue to expand the distributed architecture to meet processing needs. Capability was an issue, though, since no one seemed to know how to build distributed applications. Today, the problem is what to distribute. Some of the factors that affect the decision are:

- Interactive versus batch needs
- Capacity of existing machine resources
- Communications costs
- Requirements for availability of services
- Price/performance analysis
- Horizontal versus vertical organization.

There is no stock answer. Certain aspects of technical operations, for example, are more easily distributed than others. The main question is where to put hardware operations, communications support, systems programming, production control, and each of the other aspects of the function. Similar questions exist for applications development (data base administration, applications programming, systems analysis, systems documentation, user training, and so on), and control (security, setting priorities, standardizing tasks, personnel planning, evaluating products, and so on). While one might be willing to distribute scheduling, for example, under a complex, horizontal organizational structure, one might not be quite so willing to distribute planning and budgeting under the same structure.

Distributing functions can be an extremely effective alternative to centralized computing. Organizationally it makes sense because data entry, data integrity, and to some extent, the accuracy of reports can be assigned to units with the greatest vested interest in the quality of their information. Since admissions offices, for example, care a great deal more about socio-demographic data than do business offices, one might provide equipment, personnel resources, and full responsibility for file maintenance and accuracy of such data to the admissions office.

But if distributing responsibility for file maintenance is an effective approach to a data integrity problem then, by extension, can the responsibility for planning, budgeting, and control be distributed in response to some other problem—that of too frequent and too expensive upgrades to the central facility, for example? The answer is probably, but not simply "by extension." Each situation is unique and requires its own analysis, and the results will differ from institution to institution due to such variables as size, physical plant, the current status of technological capabilities, and financial restrictions.

The distributed computing alternative will fit into the spectrum of solutions even better in the future. Technological compatibility will always be a problem, but the issue is so well understood today that the problem has become routine. Declining costs for technology will permit universities to distribute increasing amounts of machine intelligence, and the real compatibility problems that will occur relate to the impact on management of distributing data, primarily as a result of seemingly incompatible reports generated by different offices from the same data base.

Productivity Tools

Productivity tools are computer languages designed to help programmers write programs faster. These tools can be an alternative to the conventional programming approaches. Vendors will claim that programmers, who normally average 10 to 20 lines of code per day, can increase productivity to 1,000 lines per day. Buyers might conclude that a hundredfold increase in productivity is possible, and that one ought to be able to produce new applications systems at least several times faster with productivity tools. Tools are available to assist in activities such as generating batch reports, developing sample screens and reports during systems design activities ("prototyping"), and querying on line data bases.

But conventional programming has traditionally involved many specific steps: user definitions, design, development, pre-implementation, implementation. Each step results in specific products—a technical product, user manuals, and operations documentation during the development step. The act of coding is but one part of the applications development process.

The following list presents one version of the systems development process:

Step	Results in
User definitions	Functional specifications
	Budget estimates
Design	Technical specifications
	Documentation
	Better budget estimates
Development	Technical product
	User manuals
	Operations documentation
Pre-implementation	User testing
	User training
Implementation	Turnover
	Production
	Monitoring operations

Prototyping helps, but the majority of the effort, from conception through operation, is not coding intensive. To develop applications properly requires as much attention to user training as to coding modules to update the data base. Equally important are questions such as efficiencies of machine use, response time, maintenance, and post-implementation modifications. Expectations need to be managed during the acquisition process.

A Chief Information Officer might select productivity tools for a programming staff and one of the delivery agents for a great variety of reasons. First, and perhaps most important, significant productivity gains can be obtained during certain parts of most applications. Screen generation, as one example, is easier and faster with appropriate productivity tools. End-user computing, discussed in more detail in the section on information centers, would not be possible to the extent that it is today without report generators, statistical packages, and query facilities. Finally, activities such as centrally supported ad hoc reporting, and some aspects of batch reporting, can be performed with significant increases in productivity, assuming that the correct tools have been chosen.

Information Centers

Information centers have evolved as natural consequences of both the distributing of computing and the productivity tools alternatives. Universities are clearly dealing with an expanded applications development environment, one in which programming is performed on at least three levels: traditional data center employees, information specialists (for example, budget analysts and institutional researchers), and a host of other, typically less sophisticated end-users.

End-users, however, are rapidly becoming more literate in computing because of the increased availability of microcomputers. As a result, end-users are increasingly involved in computing activities. This trend, coupled with the trend toward increased use of selected productivity tools by end-users, has significantly changed the environment in which computing and communications services are provided.

CIOs can either establish, or support, an information center or accomplish the same goals by appropriately increasing the resources allocated to user services within the existing data center. Information centers become a focus for training and consulting for end-users, similar to a traditional academic computing center.

Information centers also can help reduce applications backlogs. Ad hoc programming needs have an important effect on the amount of resources available to develop and maintain new core applications. Too many ad hoc requirements in the backlog generate such problems as slow responses to requests, delays in new systems development, and unhappy users.

An information center can reduce an applications backlog by developing policies that cause, whenever possible, initiators of ad hoc requests to learn how to develop their own reports. The argument in favor of such an approach is that centrally funded and managed resources are scarce and expensive, and may be best allocated in support of new systems implementation. It is not clear that universities continue to afford the luxury of a pool of individuals who are responsible specifically for ad hoc requests.

Whether information centers will continue to exist in their present form is not clear, although it is probable that they will. It is clearer that end-user computing will continue to expand as costs for technology continue to decline, users of technology become less difficult, and end-users of technology become increasingly more sophisticated. Information centers or their derivatives will become ever more common alternatives to direct provision of services.

Computing Services Industry

The computing services industry began in the mid 1960s and has been growing at the rate of 20 percent per year for the past decade. It exists in part because of the relative newness of the entire computing industry, in part because of needs for additional expertise on an on-demand basis, and in part because of the ability of any industry that has made significant capital investments in people and products to leverage those investments in cost-effective ways. The industry offers a range of alternatives to a CIO trying to develop the most cost-effective solution to the problems at his or her university. Products and services available include:

- Consulting
- Contract programming

- Data processing services
- Applications software
- Facilities management
- Systems-integration services.

A CIO's decision to turn to a vendor for a particular solution is almost always based either on the availability of in-house expertise or on cost, or on some combination of the two. For example, the trend toward purchasing and installing large, complex, packaged applications software rather than building it, is based on cost ratios ranging from 10 to 1 up to 100 to 1, and on time savings of up to 10 to 1. Alternatively, a decision to buy custom software is much more difficult to make because it is not nearly so clear whether there will be significant cost savings, even in light of potential time savings and possible lack of in-house expertise.

The computing service industry has evolved along with the rest of the computing industry. Increasingly, vendors offer relational data base products, products that support upload and download capabilities, and products or systems that are fully integrated into their overall product line. Vendors are increasingly interested in trends in systems integration, integrated workstations, and mission critical systems (for example, recruiting, retention, and curricula), and, to some extent, products and services are being offered in these arenas.

Universities have traditionally not adopted products from the computing services industry as rapidly as their counterparts in the private sector. Need was perhaps an inhibitor, cost another, and pride of internally developed solutions a third. Trends are weakening each of these inhibitors. As university executives become increasingly sophisticated in their applications of technology, and as those applications become increasingly complex, the tendency to depend totally on in-house solutions will probably diminish. Finally, as vendors continue to pour capital into the development of a spectrum of integrated products and services, the ability of in-house solutions to compete cost effectively will also probably diminish.

The Systems Integration Solution

Systems integration is the term being used by most CIOs for the alternative they are constructing to solve today's computing problems. Once viewed as separate entities, such things as distributed computing, communications, information centers, purchased software or services, multiple vendor hardware environments, and the other elements that make up the information resources environment of today's universities are now all considered pieces of a single puzzle. Capacity, capability, and compatibility remain key issues, but the questions are now focused at the component level rather than at the systems level. Integration of these components into one cohesive service will be the central problem of the next decade. From

Figure 1. Alternative Approaches for Services

EXAMPLES OF NEEDS	Classic Model	Distributed Functions	Productivity Tools	Information Centers	Computing Services Industry	Systems Integration Model
Develop and Manage University Data Bases	X				X	X
Support Ad Hoc Programming	X	X	X	X		X
Connect Diverse/Distributed Machine Intelligence					X	X
Control Operations, Development, Policy, etc.	X	X				X
Manage Expansion/Upgrade Cost Increments		X				X
Develop and Maintain Core Administrative Systems	X				X	X
Assign Responsibility for Data Integrity/Ownership	X	X				X
Implement Large Scale Systems	X				X	X
Conduct Large Scale Projects	X				X	X
Support End-User Computing		X	X	X		X
Support Non-Traditional Applications — E-Mail, Communicating Copiers, Office Systems, Etc.		X		X		
Reduce the Applications Backlog		X	X	X	X	X
Train and Consult Users	X			X		X

the CIO's point of view, it does not make sense to have the typical array of capacities and machine intelligence, from micros to mainframes and copiers to facsimile devices, spread throughout the university without them being able to communicate. One way to begin to increase the return on the investment that a university has made in technology is to recognize that the integrated sum of that investment is significantly greater than the accumulation of its elements.

Thirty years ago the computing center was a single entity in a discrete physical location. We now need to think of the university as our computing center, with bits and pieces of the center's machine intelligence spread throughout the university and linked together with a communications network. Communications becomes the integrator; information centers and such components as productivity tools become catalysts that distribute information.

Summary

The matrix in Figure 1 contains examples of typical university needs. The matrix indicates that neither the needs nor the alternatives form mutually exclusive subsets, and suggests the need for a systems integrated approach. Good management dictates that one should attempt to obtain the best possible return on investment, whatever its level. Alternative models for the delivery of computing and communications exist as never before, and it is becoming increasingly incumbent upon CIOs to achieve optimal efficiency by finding the best fit among university needs, available resources, and available options for the allocation of those resources.

E. Michael Staman has been involved in higher education since 1966, serving as a faculty member and in various administrative capacities in computing, institutional research, and planning.

As institutions of higher education attempt to maximize their advantages through today's converging technologies, they recognize that the tools associated with office automation are no longer those of a discrete discipline.

Developing Office and Information Center Components

Joan Day

This chapter focuses on the history, status, and outlook of office computing in colleges and universities. It reviews the technologies, the internal activities and organizational structures, and the external influences that have affected, and will continue to affect, the office computing environment in higher education. This chapter differentiates those technologies, organizations, and activities that facilitate effective solutions from those that pose obstacles to practical automation. While there is no intent to view office automation as problematic, it is helpful to examine how past and present situations have created inhibiting perceptions of the definition and role of office computing. This focus on a familiar digest of technological and situational problems leads to promising solutions.

The Situation Summary

1. Technology has undergone rapid changes and to a large degree has redefined computing needs. Desktop computing power is real and available. Distributed processing is the idea of the moment.

E. M. Staman (ed.). *Managing Information in Higher Education.*
New Directions for Institutional Research, no. 55. San Francisco: Jossey-Bass, Summer 1987.

2. Equipment acquisitions at the departmental level have skyrocketed, while computing cost analyses and return-on-investment projections and measurements are frequently not performed.

3. With better tools, it is much less expensive to quickly develop new applications. It is as difficult and costly as ever to integrate existing core systems on central computers.

4. Management information systems (MIS) organizations are gaining renewed respect and control, but with a redefined role. MIS had suffered a brief lapse of attention to end-users who rushed to solve their computing problems with desktop computing and not through MIS.

5. Office end-users are more sophisticated and computer literate than ever.

6. Central computing, office automation, and telecommunications have traditionally been organizationally segregated.

7. Faculty, administrative staff, clerical staff, and student computing have traditionally been supported by discrete support groups.

8. Telecommunications, office automation, and data processing technologies are converging.

9. Computing needs of faculty, students, administrators, and clerical staff are converging.

10. In the meantime, many institutions face decreasing enrollments and decreased funding.

The Problem Summary

1. Real computing needs are not easily distinguished from perceived needs. There are more technology alternatives to choose from than ever.

2. There is an ever-increasing base of computing end-users to support.

3. Distributed processing does not eliminate the need to integrate interdependent, centralized systems. There is still much of the old work to do.

4. The balance of responsibility between MIS and distributed processing users is not well defined; responsibility for data integrity and security, once a primary charge of central computing, is, by default, distributed throughout the organizations.

5. Office automation, because it is more than word processing, generally receives little support from professionals representing other facets of the organization's computing needs.

6. Telecommunications, because it is more than voice communications, generally receives little support from professionals representing other facets of the organization's data communication needs.

The Problem Effect Summary

1. If long-range technology planning is avoided, the confusion will continue; independent decisions resulting in major investments may not make effective use of the converging technologies.

2. If the state of technology is perceived as too confusing, no decisions may be made and the computing situation will continue to raise levels of user (including student) frustration.

3. Inadequate investments in end-user support or self-sufficiency programs will erode the potential return on investments.

4. Funding restrictions can preempt a search for cost reduction opportunities through strategic investments in technology.

The Solution Summary

1. Institutions must recognize the convergence of office, telecommunications, and data processing technologies; recognize the convergence of end-user needs; separate real needs from perceived needs through goal-oriented institutional planning; and not be hesitant to turn to independent systems-integration consultants and other institutions who have faced and addressed similar problems.

2. Some of the tactical components of the solution include appointment of a chief information officer responsible for all components of computing, including data processing, academic computing, information centers, telecommunications, office computing and implementation of the departmental information officer concept, as a way to distribute responsibility for many of the functions traditionally held by MIS alone. Other vehicles include hiring information center staff who recognize the nuances but not artificial boundaries between academic and administrative end-users; establishment of standards for all computing acquisitions that are flexible enough to anticipate exceptions, additions, and new qualifications; and end-user forums for input to the technology planning process.

3. There must be a commitment to provide new skills and technological expertise. Further, the integration of many formerly discrete entities (for example, old and new skills; MIS, academic, and administrative views; central computer and office computer tools) will create the synergy needed to escape the cycle of piecemeal and incomplete solutions.

The State of the Office

Before reviewing the current state of office components, it will be helpful to reflect on the history of the use of office technologies in higher education. This brief history, along with a discussion of office technology's internal and external influences and the effectiveness of technology until now, will allow institutions to identify the key office automation decision factors: what to maintain, what to invest in, what to develop, what to change, and what to wait for.

Use of Technology. Institutions of higher education were among the first to use the word processing capabilities of the central computer, and they were certainly among the first to put microcomputers (micros) to work. Word processing evolved as a separate technology with a separate support person or group serving a discrete user community of secretaries and office clerks.

Initially, micros were not put to work in the office; they were to be found in labs and dorms, employed primarily as an academic instruction and research tool. Micro users were also mainframe users, and the academic computing consultants supported faculty and students with this new technology in much the same way they supported use of central computers.

Central computers have always provided services for both the administrative system and academic computing users. Most institutions that attempted to add word processing users to timesharing computers have since abandoned that decision. Heavy use of word processing severely slowed down everyone's use of the computer.

Technology-driven institutions invested early in either dedicated word processing equipment, shared systems that allowed multiple typists to share the intelligence, or the storage media and printers for the system. In a word processing center or pool environment, which is by nature a controlled production environment, such solutions continue to be cost effective and productive. In a highly distributed environment where secretaries and administrative personnel from different departments or different physical locations use shared resource systems, the results are often less effective. Many institutions have found the ongoing costs to manage shared resources and to maintain acceptable performance of shared-resource systems is high (often higher than the initial equipment investment). The additional costs resulted from the need to train and commit personnel to manage a very dynamic technical and procedural environment. Other costs resulted from unanticipated upgrades needed to accommodate a constantly changing base of secretarial end-users and such needs as determining the proper physical placement of a shared printer when office changes take place.

Today, the word processor of choice is the microcomputer, most commonly called the personal computer; in most cases these microcomputers are not networked together. However, more than half of all institutions with central administrative computers are linking their microcomputers to the central mainframe.

When discussing the use of technology in the office, we must include the use of the administrative systems of the organization. Access to the central data base information is key to office efficiency, and ultimately, to the delivery of quality student services. Clerical staff deal with maintaining the computer-based records of the institution, either by using a terminal or microcomputer to update the data base directly, or by hand-posting transactions later processed by the computing center personnel. The secretary, the data clerk, and the office administrators all need access to records.

Viewing the administrator as an office computing user, let us examine this knowledge worker's use of the personal computer. In institutions of higher education, the knowledge workers are those who use data for decision-support purposes. Budget directors, institutional research officers, and administrative deans are primary examples. In use are such software tools as electronic spreadsheets for work plan and budget maintenance, activity tracking, and projections. This user may also employ the microcomputer to access central or external computer systems, to do his or her own correspondence and report drafts, or to send messages through electronic mail systems, and may develop presentation materials that combine graphics and text.

Faculty are not typically regarded as members of the office community, but indeed they are, and they do use office productivity tools. The very nature of the research faculty member's work maximizes the investment in electronic mail systems; they provide access to colleagues throughout the institution and throughout the country. Whether the faculty members are involved in research, public service, publishing, or instruction, they also use or will benefit from using computers for the same basic purposes as the administrator: word processing, presentation material production, information access, and data analysis.

Influence of Technology. The introduction of desktop computing met with notably different receptions. It caused users to become hopeful and challenged, vendors to seize the sales opportunity, and many MIS departments to initially discount the potential of personal computing.

As a result of this mixed reception the office component of information management enjoys an important distinction from traditional computing systems: development of the office component typically did not originate with MIS departments. By providing tools that allow end-users to be their own MIS professionals, office automation tools, especially the personal computer, have ostensibly freed the office administrators and their staff from the control of the MIS department. The real challenge has been to apply the same principles of information management practiced by MIS professionals for decades. As we follow some of the other significant influences of blossoming technology, we will see that the growth of influence and control indicates that we can maximize distributed office computing potential.

The desktop technology vendors saw the opportunity to deal with a new set of customers: the end-users in the office. These vendors capitalized on the notion that much of what was once accomplished on central computers is now available on the desktop. They marketed desktop power. They recognized that the benefits of functions such as word processing and spreadsheet analysis were obvious and attractive to potentially every office in the institution. In addition, everyone in the institution wanted a personal office computer.

Most importantly, these new customers influenced vendors in a way that MIS and data processing departments never did. In the beginning of the personal computer era, there was no need to sell to the MIS director; the MIS directors were, in fact, avoided. They were viewed as an obstacle, often insisting that PCs could not begin to solve the current backlog of system deficiencies and new user requests. Vendors saw what the MIS director did not. The users were ready to take matters into their own hands. For the first time, vendors were hearing directly what the users wanted, not what MIS wanted or what MIS said the users wanted. As a result of this direct user influence, today's hardware or software vendor considers the following to be principles for success: *user friendly, integrated, compatible,* and *standard.*

Many MIS departments had been restricted by the high costs of maintenance and development in the mainframe environment from adopting these principles of success. Ironically, the initial lack of standards and compatibility among PC and distributed processing systems was one of the major reasons MIS personnel became activists in the PC revolution. It was not the only reason, however.

Organizations recognized that individual office acquisitions needed to be justified in terms not only of the objectives of the department, but the overall computing and computing-support goals of the organization. Both MIS and institution administrators realized that the cost of computing was not reflected in the MIS budget alone. MIS departments were asked to bring order and accountability to the office equipment acquisition process. They were also asked to implement computer literacy programs. As a result, MIS regained its primary influence and is, once again, one of the primary clients that vendors must satisfy.

The promises of the personal computer and office computing have clearly shown the need for the experience and support of MIS organizations. But other external influences of technology will soon touch higher education in a similarly demanding way. Secondary schools, on one hand, are sending students to college with great expectations. Industry, on the other hand, has great expectations of the college graduate. In both cases, it is the wide exposure to office computing tools that rightfully creates the demands of higher education to continue to build on the student's understanding and use of the computer as a tool in virtually every discipline and career preparation program offered.

Now, many colleges and universities are planning to maximize their competitive advantage through the potential of today's converging technologies. As they do, they are recognizing that the tools associated with office automation are no longer those of a discrete discipline. They are understanding that, while word processing, desktop publishing, personal computer-based spreadsheet and data base programs, electronic mail, local area networks, and other office technologies are specialized and targeted for the office end-user, these technologies are becoming increasingly integrated with such traditional technologies as voice communications and "back office" administrative computing systems. Furthermore, the technologies can be integrated and employed from a single desktop device. Given the potential to integrate all types of computing, the application and management of office automation technology is converging with the other, more mature, components of information management. In the same way, the basic computing needs of faculty and administrators are converging. Universities and colleges must now seriously consider appointment of a chief information officer, responsible for all components of computing and information processing.

The Efficacy of Technology. The blame for imperfect solutions is often placed on equipment and software deficiencies. Most failures are the result of not knowing the limitations of a technology, and of inadequate planning, training, and resources to support and manage the automated work environment.

The question is really not whether technology has measured up. It is whether institutions have committed, knowledgeable support staff who understand both computing and the goals of the organization and who provide the framework and guidelines for users and offices to determine complete and effective solutions. We must also ask whether there has been a commitment to provide support resources to ensure the ongoing effectiveness of automation solutions. If an institution understands but is not driven by technology, and if one of the programmatic goals of automation is to build user self-sufficiency, then technology can produce the desired results. To illustrate the point, here is a discussion of some typical office automation technologies along with some typical perceived needs followed by examples of how implementations may not have been successful.

Document Interchange. The need for this capability was created when organizations invested in incompatible word processors and personal computing equipment and software. Once accustomed to the advantages of word processing, users did not want to be told they were limited to using only one kind of machine or that their secretary could not continue to edit as usual. The need grew to encompass document distribution and library (document access) services, so that what was once disseminated on paper could be delivered electronically, from workstation to workstation. While many organizations invested in products that provided the technical solution to the incompatibility problem, many did not assess who could benefit most from the capability. Often the most appropriate users did not have or were not budgeted to have the proper workstations, communication links, printers, and training in the procedures and rules that governed a successful (that is, that saved some people time or money) document interchange or transfer.

Local Area Networks. Once personal computers are in place, the natural desire is to tie them together so that software, printers, and applications can be shared. Often "sharing" becomes the sole justification for a network implementation. All the technical considerations, such as the type of cables needed and the network software and hardware requirements, are evaluated and an implementation is planned. The applications that are to be shared may include word processing, spreadsheet analysis, and access to a new multiple-user system (a stores inventory system, for example). The plan is also to share printers and disk file storage.

The decision to develop the inventory system may have been what appeared to be a good, cost-effective use of this latest and greatest technology; the rationale was that, after all, the PCs were already there and tying them together made sense. There may have been no consideration of the alternative to develop the inventory system on the university's central administrative computer, where perhaps it could be designed with greater flexibility, to provide access to other departments in the institution, and to be integrated with accounts payable and work-order systems already in place. How could such an alternative be overlooked? It happens when decisions are made independently by the department or if the consultant, a PC support specialist from the university's information center, for example, is not aware of other systems and other departments who may want to share the benefits of an on line stores inventory system.

Desktop publishing, artificial intelligence/expert systems, voice/video interfaces, optical scanners/optical disks are all technologies that come to mind when office automation or office computing is mentioned. Each is a technology that requires expertise; each holds promise for educational institutions. How the expertise and application of these technologies are developed is a challenge with which the computing services organization must deal.

The State of the Computing Services Organization

One impact of evolving technologies and more sophisticated users is a need for MIS organizations to develop new skills and deal with new responsibilities. In most universities, clear definitions and a merging of responsibilities have yet to be established. Historically, computing-support departments tend to organize either by discrete automation function or by discrete user group. For example, administrative systems groups support administrative users, office automation specialists support word processing, and academic consultants support faculty and students. The total automation needs of any one user cannot be satisfied with this type of support structure. This is evidenced by the increased number of users who have made their own automation equipment decisions and, by default, often painfully acquired the skills and attendant information-management responsibilities.

The views that are brought to bear from the MIS group, from the information center group, and from the user community are necessary for satisfactory solutions for the individual department and to the organization itself. The institutions that provide a forum to consider and evaluate all the views of the aforementioned groups are more likely to achieve complete and compatible solutions; and more likely to avoid a mismatch of training investments to the actual skills required throughout the organization.

There are many independent groups providing many different types of technical support and advice to many discrete constituencies in most institutions today. There are many "experts"; there could be more sharing of expertise. There could be more education at all levels, from executives to staff personnel. As much as users may feel disengaged from MIS, most will admit they are still striving to make optimal use of their equipment or software.

Perhaps the most positive influence of the vast inventory of current and potential investments in technology is the fact that it will encourage organizations to make automation investment and management decisions based on the common goals of the institution. Currently, most office investment decisions are technically sound, but not always broadly focused and not necessarily inclusive of the proper training and ongoing support available.

Office Automation Challenges: Who Owns Them?

A Need for Ongoing Evaluation. All institutions must evaluate the return on the investments made in technology. If technology is mistrusted, it is usually because the ability to optimize it is mistrusted. An evaluation process will clearly produce optimal results. A plan to evaluate is a plan to succeed, because business or academic goals are used as the measure.

Evaluation programs are, of necessity, functions of specific environments, but there are a number of elements common to all environments, and most of these elements can, and should be measured. Examples include user satisfactions and productivity, and achievement of departmental service goals. The services of a support organization that should be evaluated, such as an information center, include analysis, training, implementation, and system administration and problem support.

Finally, the business goals of the department or office should be established and measured by the department whether the department is automated or not. By their nature, service organizations should set their own service goals and should be evaluated both internally and by the end-users.

Imperfect Technology. The institution's challenge includes being able to know when a technology is mature enough to be truly useful and cost effective. We previously discussed some of the problems with burgeoning and alluring technologies. Organizations often choose to develop their own tools. We cannot forget that academic research institutions may quite properly contribute to the emergence and maturity of a technology within their own research and development purview. The administrative side of the house should at once want to solicit academic opinion and advice. The benefits of a unique combination of natural process (found in institutions of learning) and cost-conscious planning (found in every accountable organization) can be leveraged through the cooperative efforts of research faculty and administrative computing planners. But institutions must be sure that organizational goals are the driving force.

Technology assessments have traditionally been charged to the MIS department. There is more reason than ever for this responsibility to remain with MIS. What must change are the evaluation criteria. These must, in large part, come from the office user community. Technology will provide "perfect" results only when the end-users are part of the assessment, selection, and implementation process.

Solutions for the Competitive Academic Institution

Planning: An Interdisciplinary Approach. What part does development of the office component play in the grand scheme of harnessing computing and communication technologies? Because technology directly offers so much to the office environment, the office may soon be mapping its own future.

Institutions cannot meet organizational objectives through technology alone, through MIS alone, through a single vendor solution, and certainly not through multiple independent departmental decisions. However, office computing must be the backbone of any pragmatic approach for planning across all forms of technology. The individual department plays a major role in establishing the business goals that become the criteria for technology investment or divestment decisions.

The mission of an office computing planning effort should be to establish a plan and an organization to address the common goals of each office and the unique and important goals of individual offices. The plan should be strategic, business (or competition) oriented, and flexible enough to accommodate administrative organization changes and the special needs of self-supporting units. It should also recognize the ramifications of technology advances, such as the need to plan for replacement of typewriters, copiers, and publications equipment.

The planning process should include a mechanism to ensure that common office functions owned by a specific organizational unit are identified as standard as well as common. An example is the publishing function. If several departments are producing publication materials that are ultimately channeled through the publications department for final productions, and contributing offices are considering using desktop publishing software, the automation solution for each department should be standardized. In contrast, if publications are not being filtered through the publications department, today's publishing technology provides an opportunity to consider centralized management of the publishing function, with copy production distributed to the authoring departments.

Another example is the records management function. If the institution has a records management or archives department, the policies and procedures established by that department should influence the automated records management function of each office. Problems common to both hard-copy file cabinets and electronic files include file overflow, secure back-up and storage of vital documents, and file location. The rules for efficient filing are often overlooked by computer users. Records management departments are an experienced source of knowledge not to be overlooked when electronic document management procedures are developed for all office computer users. There will be unique departmental goals that do not impact and are not impacted by other departments. In such cases, exceptions to established standards may be made, but the criteria for exceptions must be clear.

Because of the new knowledge and understanding of computing capabilities, and because of the self-sufficiency being experienced in offices that have employed some form of automation, the office administrator and the knowledge workers in such offices have significantly more to contribute to the information management planning process than ever before. If an institution has never had a viable computing task force, composed of MIS staff, information center staff, and members from every end-user constituency, now is a most critical time to start one.

Organization: An Information Management Approach. There are three relatively new organizational concepts that contribute positively to the development of the office computing component. They are the chief information officer, departmental information officers, and a new kind of information center. What is new about the concept of a chief information officer is that this person is responsible for all computing constituencies and all technologies that deal with information processing, including telecommunications. Departmental information officers are representatives of discrete organizational units. Their responsibilities include establishing the information processing and automation goals of their unit; assuming primary ownership of the definition, use, and security of the data generated and maintained by their unit; and representing the goals and needs of their unit in the computing planning process. The difference between this information officer and what are now commonly called user representatives or liaisons is that he or she is official, having not just responsibilities, but authority and accountability.

The new information center is one that serves all computing end-users. It is staffed with personnel knowledgeable not only in the new office technologies but also in the traditional technologies and application systems. This center is committed to a primary goal of establishing user self-sufficiency. It works with and leverages the skills of other computing center technicians and programmers in its capacity as the single point of reference for user support. Its primary function is to educate.

Conclusion

While the development of the office component is not an easy task, we hope to have made the case for viewing it as the foundation for, and not just another form of, computing in universities and colleges.

It was promised earlier that we might better understand what to maintain, what to invest in, what to develop, what to change, and what to wait for. Institutions should strive to maintain what is now working well. Colleges and universities should invest in people, the development of new skills, the integration of experiences and new skills, and adequately staffed information centers. They must develop plans and organization structures that share and apply common goals. Self-sufficiency among computing users must be developed, as must guidelines for what is rightfully an office computing function versus a mainframe computer function.

Higher-education institutions must change the role of the MIS director from that of a director of technology experts and processing centers to a key member of the administration. The MIS director must represent the university or college mission as any of its vice-presidents would. So, too, must the role of any of the end-user be changed to one of greater accountability and self-sufficiency.

Finally, colleges and universities should assess each automation venture using a phased implementation approach and should test, prototype, and measure each office computing venture before going on to the next technology or the next office.

Joan Day is the director of Office Automation Services at Systems and Computer Technology Corporation (SCT). Her responsibilities have included on-site management at client accounts and consulting services for community colleges, proprietary schools, and universities. Prior to joining SCT in 1983, she served as the manager of Administrative Systems Programming and End-User Services at the University of Delaware Computing Center.

Changes in academic computing threaten to change the nature of higher education institutions, including their most fundamental activity—classroom instruction.

Academic Computing: The Challenges Ahead

Stanley Warren

In the past decade, academic computing in higher education institutions has moved from the arcane to the mundane. Once a resource physically separated from those who used it, the computer has emerged from the data processing center to take its place among faculty and students as a potent learning tool. Formerly serving a limited range of instructional functions requiring a large, complex system, educational computing today has found a home on faculty and student desktops, using relatively simple machines running easily operated software at increasingly lower costs.

This evolution, or even revolution, in learning techniques poses a major challenge to the academic community: Having brought the computer into the college, how can the college now be put on the computer?

To understand the scope of this challenge, one must trace the development of academic computing from its inception to its current state—somewhat akin to a rapidly growing and difficult to manage child. Good parents that we educators are, we look at this enfant terrible and wonder what we must do to help it into the future that will transform us all.

If one affirmatively answers the question posed by Harvard president Derek Bok in 1985 of whether the computer is a genuine development in education or a short-lived fad, then one faces the challenge of integrating a major technology into a traditional institution. At the same time,

E. M. Staman (ed.). *Managing Information in Higher Education.*
New Directions for Institutional Research, no. 55. San Francisco: Jossey-Bass, Summer 1987.

not only the institution of higher education must be transformed physically and operationally, but classroom instruction and the role of the teacher who delivers that instruction must be redefined.

As complex and difficult as the reconstitution of higher education will be as we move into the next century, the task is further complicated by a change in the very nature of the human psyche, involving a shift away from verbal conceptualization into a new, vaguer world of visual imagery and verbal approximation that has an even greater impact on learning than technology. The English historian Arnold Toynbee maintained that societies grow and flourish when faced by challenge. If the challenge is too severe to be met, the society dies from overexertion; if there is no challenge, the society just as surely dies from inactivity. The challenge posed by academic computing is of the kind that will allow our society to continue to develop. To do so, however, will require a substantial investment of mental energy and resources.

Demystification of Academic Computing

When the computer first arrived at colleges and universities in the early 1960s, it was a physically large and bulky machine prone to erratic performance, requiring the attention of a considerable number of highly technical professionals. These programmers and operators had complicated duties, that required many hours to perform and were very difficult for the layperson to understand. In the beginning, the machines and those who tended them were segregated from the rest of the institution, and for educational purposes were made available to faculty on a very limited and highly specialized basis. This early form of academic computing was well under way by 1970, and through the 1970s was "the nature of the beast." This characterization was changed by the emergence of the microcomputer, which put an end to the mainframe computer as the dominant mode of instructional technology.

Before the age of miniaturization, however, a college or university wanting to obtain and use a computing machine had to create and maintain a separate facility to house the hardware and the numerous staff needed to operate it. From this need was born the computer center, a discrete academic support facility of the type represented by its elder cousin, the library.

The machine operated in a machine room, which had to be a climate-controlled environment. The hardware components of this mainframe computer were all large in size and included not only the processor, but card readers, disk drives, tape drives, printers, video display terminals to monitor the various software systems, and communications machines that enabled the other devices to interact with each other.

To operate the data processing system, several operators tended the many hardware devices and issued commands to the system. Installation of new functions, or applications, required the efforts of a substantial number of programmers, who wrote thousands of lines of code to effect a given task.

Thus it is no surprise that the original uses of the computer for instructional support were quite limited. Jobs were complex and took several days to run, and were in the hands of technical computing professionals (not educators) who knew much about the machines and software, but nothing about the subjects on which those machines and software were intended to shed light. Educators often found it difficult to intelligibly communicate to the technicians ideas on how to further use the computer in the classroom, while the technicians often found it equally difficult to make the educators aware of the technical capabilities of the computer.

In the earliest days of academic computing, two basic instructional support tasks were entrusted to the computer: the running of computing language programs as part of data processing courses, and the running of statistical programs to support various courses requiring the processing of large amounts of data using complex statistical processes. Both these activities adapted very well to batch processing, which involved running jobs at set times when the machine was available. Between the competition for machine time with other batched jobs and the all-too-frequent periods of down time caused by the many failures to which such a complicated system was prone, output from academic computing jobs submitted after one class would often not be available for the next class.

During the 1970s, various other forms of academic computing gradually appeared. The potential to use the machine to ask students questions and to discriminate between right or wrong answers was recognized early on, as was the possibility of using the machine as a kind of super-typewriter, with correctional capabilities that far outstripped those of the typewriter.

Development of Interactive Systems and Computing Labs

As interactive systems evolved, in which input was immediately processed and output directly relayed to the terminal or workstation, computing facilities or "labs" came into existence. These labs characterized the typical college data processing facility at the beginning of the 1980s. The capability for immediate feedback on academic computing activities fueled the expanding use of computing technology, moving it out of the computer center and distributing it around the campus in the form of rooms containing large numbers of terminals linked to a large computer. Whereas batch processing typically took a day for output to be returned, the development of more sophisticated, complex, and powerful operating systems made it possible for a mainframe computer to handle many jobs at once, a phenomenon sometimes termed multiprogramming. Thus more than one user at a time could submit a job to the computer and receive output return in a matter of seconds directly on a terminal screen.

The value of the increased presence of computers is indisputable. Direct access to the computer enables students to receive hands-on exposure to their subjects of study. In the study of computing science, they can program in any of several computing languages, using job control languages to learn the ins and outs of operating systems functions as well. Other academic subject applications can conveniently be grouped into two areas: (1) learning support, in which the same application can be used in any of a number of subjects; and (2) course support, in which the application is used in a particular subject or even in a particular course.

One of the earliest uses of this interactive mode for learning support was word processing—in terms of text production, truly a "better mousetrap." The rate of entering text on a word processor is similar to the capabilities of its predecessor, the typewriter. But in the realm of text editing, the power of the word processor is to the typewriter what the electric light bulb to the kerosene lamp. Students now could sit at a video display terminal and write more efficiently, whether in literature, sociology, or finance.

The principle of more efficient alteration of information was applied next to a different area, but one of equal significance in a large number of subjects: the financial statement, or balance sheet. The electronic spreadsheet combines the ease-of-change of word processing with the technology of numerical information processing first available in the calculator. The spreadsheet allows information to be placed in locations, or cells, which can identify the significance of the numerical data as written labels, can be absolute numerical values themselves, or can contain formulas that generate values in given cells according to the values in other cells and their relationships as determined by the formula. As a result, if a value is changed in a given cell on a spreadsheet, alterations are made in all other cells in which that given cell value is an element in a formula. Immediately the spreadsheet found a home in accounting and finance courses, but also began to be used in a number of other related subject areas, from banking to microeconomics to home economics.

Both word processing and spreadsheets focus on the processing of information, but developments in computing software began to improve the means of access to the information to be processed. The development of the data base, a systematic organization and storage of information, with the means to efficiently retrieve that information, was soon put to work in support of learning. Chemistry students could now store formulas, and history students could store documents. Moreover, where both word processing and spreadsheets generally are used by individuals, data bases could be created by instructors for the common use of entire classes.

Data bases offer another feature not shared by word processing or spreadsheets. They not only exist on college computers, but data bases exist externally, on large computers owned and made available by a variety of vendors. Thus, it is possible, through telecommunications, to access such materials as the catalogue of the Library of Congress, the financial and related information offered by Dow Jones, or even citations of case law in legal libraries of a size and scope well beyond those in most colleges and universities.

Use of Computer Assisted Instruction

All these software applications provide techniques that help students to learn many different subjects. The second category of academic computing is that of course-specific material, which generically has been termed computer assisted instruction (CAI). This takes several forms: drill and practice, tutorials, and testing and scoring.

In all its present aspects, CAI has already created a different style if not form of learning. Perhaps its most valuable feature is that it allows individual learning, that is, each student can go through the on line lessons at a different rate. For example, a CAI course designed for a six-month duration might take one student three months to complete, while another student might need eight months. By not placing all students in a classroom and exposing them to the same material at the same time for only that one time, CAI allows the learning to be self-paced. This feature of CAI has made it especially helpful in the area of remediation, where learning is structured on an individual (non-classroom) basis.

In the area of course-specific uses, the computer allows two related activities that have equal impact on the future of CAI: simulation and modeling software. Simulations and models exploit the strengths of the computer as a form of instructional technology, using its ability to process input and output immediate feedback, presenting the results of the data provided by the student and how the student manipulates that data.

Simulations enable students to create situational realities and are particularly well-suited to the social sciences. A student can function as a presidential candidate, a general in the Civil War, a bank president, or a marketing vice-president, and, faced with problems or tasks posed by the simulation software, can attempt to resolve or complete them. Class groups can compete against each other, as campaign staffs, military staffs, or rival companies selling the same product, and learn from their decisions and the consequences of those decisions.

Models enable students to create physical realities, whether a chemical molecule, a cubic cross-section of an ocean current, or an entire galaxy viewed over a period of millions of years! The visual images produced by models provide the same quality of feedback as the numerical or verbal data of the simulation.

Using both types of software, students can discuss the outcomes of their efforts with the instructor and with one another. They can change the parameters and explore the various "what if's" that confront them, testing the worth and validity of different approaches or solutions. The dynamic interaction with information, rather than the passive attempt merely to absorb the information, reinforces the learning that goes on.

One of the limitations to the use of simulations and models was that they belonged in the classroom, unlike CAI, which was a kind of course-specific homework that could be done in the computer lab. It took the development and proliferation of the microcomputer to bring academic computing software into the classroom, allowing exploitation of the full potential of simulations and modeling software.

Changing Face of Academic Computing

Microcomputers have had an additional impact on academic computing, fueling its exponential growth. Mainframe-based interactive computing freed instructional technology from the grip of the technicians in the computer center and brought it into the computing lab. Microcomputers have liberated educational computing from the lab and extended it into the classroom and into students' lives in dormitories, libraries, and homes.

One beneficial effect of the micro explosion has been to reduce the physical and fiscal burdens placed on higher education institutions to support this learning technology. With microcomputers, it is no longer necessary to dedicate the space and money to house workstations supervised by a staff. Although most micros in education today have been housed in traditional computing labs and managed by paid staff, the size and number of these facilities can and will be limited by physical and economic constraints. As prices drop and processing power rises, students will obtain their own smaller, lighter, and highly portable microcomputers, which will be used as combination typewriters, notebooks, and textbooks all in one.

This view of the coming role of the microcomputer shifts the focus to the future, and only hints at the changes to come in education. In the next decade and a half the very nature of education will be changed, as educators grasp and exploit the capabilities of this no longer new, but not yet fully used tool—the computer.

The computer represents as fundamental a change in education as those created by the invention of books and printing, and by the creation of the public school in the mid 1500s; changes that have endured and have shaped the very forms under which learning occurs. Each year more and more students arrive at college, already having been exposed to the computer. Often this exposure occurs in high school; but in greater and greater numbers it has occurred in elementary school. Their teachers also have received some form of training in this new technology, minimally in workshops of varying duration, in separate training courses measured in weeks, and in some cases, in college-level computing courses.

By the mid 1990s, virtually all students in colleges will have been exposed to the computer and gained some degree of competency (a term preferred over literacy). This computing competency can be defined as the ability to use a system—hardware and software—to accomplish a desired task. This development in turn will reduce, and even eliminate, the need to develop computing competencies in students on the college level (except in the form of remediation), and allow a greater focus on the use of the computer for education itself. Students and teachers will function on a base level of knowledge, with the ability to use new hardware and software as it becomes available with the same ease as new textbooks have been used.

Perhaps the most significant development in microtechnology in the past three years has been in the realm of connectibility: the ability to link microcomputers to each other, to mainframe computers, and to computers in remote sites as far away as the other side of the globe. These networks of low-cost, high-capacity microcomputers will form the basis of educational technology in the years to come.

Linking microcomputers electronically extends the reach of the teacher in the classroom, allowing on line material to be simultaneously accessed by students as part of instruction. But that reach can be extended far beyond the classroom to other classrooms on the campus, to other campuses within the institution, and to other institutions. Using electronic links, one teacher can address thousands of students at the same time.

Changes in computing programs, both in operating systems and in applications programs, will have an even greater impact on instructional computing than the hardware changes. Microcomputers can be used anywhere: banks, factories police departments, or in schools. But the software that runs on microcomputers must be specific to the tasks performed within that institution, whether it is issuing a loan, improving an invention, identifying a criminal suspect, or educating a would-be physicist. By being able to instruct people in the home or workplace, more people will be able to obtain educations, freed of the necessity to spend time in travel. More important, perhaps, it is the fact that if instructional materials have to be transferred from the medium of the printed page to the computer disk, many educators will have the opportunity to rework and improve some of that material.

Lower costs are making a computer-aided education cheaper to obtain as well. As for the microcomputer itself, software prices have plummeted from year to year. Not more than three years ago, a spreadsheet cost a minimum of $150. Today, it can be bought for $20. The same trend applies to word processing packages and data bases. In fact, all three software applications, fundamental modes of computing uses, have been combined into low-cost integrated packages, perfectly suited to student use. Not surprisingly, these functions are the three basic applications of nonspecific course support (along with statistical packages, themselves also greatly reduced in cost, from a typical price of about $250 a few years ago, to packages available at $25 today).

Of equal importance are simulations—not too long ago in their infancy and now still only in their early childhood. They have begun to realize their potential as the harbingers of the new educational software that will characterize course curricula to an increasing degree in the future. For example, in a traditional setting a political science instructor teaching a course on presidential elections might select one or more of Theodore H. White's *Making of the President* series as textbooks, or some analogous works about recent national campaigns. The students would read the books, take examinations on the material contained in the books and in the instructor's lectures, and would write a term paper, no doubt analyzing an election on their own. Certainly this traditional methodology would achieve the desired result of educating the students about the mechanics of presidential campaigning, and the history of recent races.

Using a simulation costing $50, available on the market since 1983 and requiring a relatively small amount of computer memory to run, that same instructor can involve the class as a campaign staff, with students serving as candidates, campaign managers, national, regional, and local (state) advertising managers, and managers of campaign swings. As candidates and staffs the students can decide such questions faced by their real-life counterparts as: Should the candidate take a trip abroad? Should advertising focus on doubtful states, on a case-by-case basis? Should the candidate concentrate appearances in states with a slim lead, or in states with slim deficits? and How much attention should be paid to "safe" states? More important, having made the decisions, students match their decisions against those of the opposing camp, and submit those calls to the computer, which, using the simulation software, forecasts a new electoral vote split. By "election day," when the final vote is tallied, the students have not only learned about the mechanics of presidential election campaigns, they have experienced them. The meaning of this shift in learning approach takes on new depth when the shift from learning as cognition to learning as thinking and feeling is considered. The immediacy of experiential learning provided by simulations increases the effectiveness of classroom activities to an extent not possible with more traditional learning forms. It is the difference between reading about riding a bicycle and riding it oneself.

In such a setting, the role of the instructor alters from a provider of learning to a facilitator for learning. It becomes the instructor's task not only to teach the class, but to select the software and ensure that the students can properly interpret some of the strategies appropriate to the simulation. Some of the instructor's facilitating activities would take place on line, on a master microcomputer or mainframe terminal, networked or linked to student slave micros or terminals. The shift in emphasis from being just a provider to also being a facilitator could free faculty to do more research and to avail themselves of the computing resources used by their students.

Use of software in the classroom goes beyond instructional activities and involves support functions as well. Attendance can be taken, tests administered and scored, and final grades calculated and posted—techniques already in use in many institutions today. What remains is for those functions to be integrated with supplementary instructional materials. For example, there is no reason to discard written information altogether; it can easily be entered into the data base, and accessed and read by students on the screen, in addition to dictionaries, encyclopedias, and other reference materials already available. As a final step, electronic notebooks can be created for students to record their notes on line, where they can be stored and reaccessed as desired. Although all these functions can be performed separately in separate media, savings in cost and efficiency can be achieved through consolidation on the computer.

Some educational software and the aforementioned instructional techniques already exist in the classroom, though rather haphazardly. One class uses a simulation, another an on line dictionary. What is needed, and what already has occurred in the area of hardware, is a top-down redesigning of the higher education process to use this plethora of academic computing resource in a coherent, consistent manner. Restructured in this way, the institution of higher education would be quite energy efficient, as futurists have pointed out. In courses using simulations, classrooms would be needed, but many other educational activities could be carried on through remote access from students' homes or dorm rooms. The resulting smaller physical facilities would require less energy for heating and cooling than present facilities, less fuel would be needed to transport students to and from the campus. Smaller facilities would be easier to maintain, and hence more economical in other respects as well—a vital consideration in this era of reduced governmental support.

In addition to the modeling power of software, which allows chemists to design new substances and biologists to create new genetic mutations, software exists that can analyze the style and content of Shakespeare's works and match texts by contemporary authors against those parameters. Pictographic languages from Assyrian to Mayan can undergo the powerful scrutiny of a computing program with graphics capabilities that can accommodate these ancient languages, increasing the ability of scholars to decipher them and opening past worlds to our understanding. This is not to suggest that any of the human elements—teachers as socializers, bearers of culture, and even as figures of inspiration—could or should be undermined by the creation of computerized instructional materials.

The next step in the process would be to package all the software needed to support a given course and put it on line. The hardware technology already exists to store, retrieve, and process this material, and to make it available to students on campus and at home. Electronic schools already exist, but their software is still the very limited drill and practice material accompanied by tutorials—techniques that are twenty years old or more. The on line courses of the future would be a generation more sophisticated than the traditional modes of computerized learning materials. Also, unlike the individual packages in use in classes today, they would be all-inclusive, containing all the materials needed for a grasp of the course's subject matter.

This stage would be followed by the creation of entire curricula on line: major subject courses, and related minors and electives, which together would constitute fulfillment of degree requirements in a particular subject area. This is the great challenge facing instructional designers in the next ten years. The techniques for integration of learning activities within a software package for a given course already exist; the actual developmental activities remain to be implemented. But to create an entire module of on line courses that will satisfy the academic requirements of certifying agencies in fifty states, gaining the support of educational administrators and faculty alike, is a Herculean task.

On line curriculum is possible, but entails use of a wide range of computing resources. In addition to the simulations designed for many courses, text materials would have to be selected and supplemented by on line catalogue to identify and locate other materials not immediately available on the computer. The subsequent assembling of these materials within an operating system to regulate access and use of the programs, is itself a major software engineering task. Thus both the form of the on line curriculum and its content would require substantial commitments of time, money, and the skills of sophisticated data processing professionals. With knowledge of the ingredients, the task that lies ahead is to combine them in order to create an on line university that could characterize higher education into the next century.

One means for increasing use of computing in instruction might be to create a think tank, consisting of education and computing experts working in tandem. The modality by which such a think tank could function can be termed a *higher education institute,* existing within the framework of a larger organizational entity, though perhaps physically separate. The staff of the institute would first and foremost consist of subject matter experts, probably drawn from the faculty of existing colleges and universities. These individuals would be recognized scholars with a broad grasp of their materials, but at the same time would be working teachers with a depth of classroom instructional experience. The computing experts would be competent in the latest software technology, particularly in the area of course-authoring languages, expert systems, and graphics. They would also understand operating systems techniques, as well as the capabilities of hardware, and particularly of networked microcomputers.

Coordinating the efforts of the two types of experts would be less-specialized individuals with competencies in both areas. These instructional designers would serve as conduits, conveying the requirements of subject matter to the technicians, and the capabilities of the technologies to the academics. These coordinators also would address the quality control question of academic certification, and would focus on the political issues that arise from presenting traditional educational institutions with a new form of instruction.

The courseware developed by this design team would meet the academic goal of improved instructional results arising from participatory learning. It would fully exploit both the hardware and software technologies, and no doubt would lead to the development of new forms of both. Depending on the relationship of the institute to the mother academic institution, modules of this courseware could be tested within the framework of existing courses, and entire classes in a specific subject area could later be automated.

At the same time, accreditation could be sought for the institute for non-matriculating students, similar to that already attained by "electronic colleges" in existence today, which offer correspondence school courses using new hardware technology. The institute's courses would be held within the physical confines of the facility, and would serve as tests for the automated courses developed by the instructional design team.

While these developmental activities were taking place, and while the issue of accreditation was being resolved, an implementation plan would be devised for use by existing, traditional higher education institutions desiring to incorporate on line curriculum. Such a plan would envision a gradual integration of the on line curriculum, occurring in two phases. The first phase would take about three years, being the time during which the first on line course was designed (that is, customized for the curriculum in that particular institution), tested in a pilot section, and then extended to the remaining sections of that course. In the second phase, extending approximately twelve years beyond the completion of the first, the remaining courses within that curriculum would be converted to on line instruction. An institution undertaking such an endeavor in 1990 would thus begin the next century using then-current technologies.

Such an effort would involve a commitment of substantial resources from the beginning, before any financial benefits are derived from a conversion of instructional technology. To do so well beyond the financial capabilities of most higher education institutions, and as a result they probably will have to look to foundations or to the private sector to form a partnership in the transformation of instruction.

There are many types of companies that would naturally be possible partners in the creation of a higher education institute. Manufacturers of computing hardware and software already participate with colleges and universities in a wide range of joint activities. The efforts focus primarily on elaborating the reach of computing hardware, and developing uses for educational software in the traditional mode (that is, within the course, and not as the course). Other possible corporate partners in reengineering educational techniques would be firms operating computing facilities for educational and other institutions, and companies that specialize in training, using computer-based materials and techniques.

In a partnership venture, the preferable physical location would be on campus, but with the proviso that dedicated, up-to-date computing hardware would be available. Faculty would be drawn from the participating institution, probably taking leaves from their regular assignments. The partner corporation would supply the computing expertise through personnel assigned from other duties or hire for the project. The instructional designers, coordinating the efforts of the two groups, could be recruited from any of three sources: the college, the corporation, or the job market. The equipment and software to be used would be provided by the company, while the operating costs of the physical facilities would either be borne by the corporation, the college, or both, depending on where the institute was located.

Conclusion

The potential of an on line university or college in terms of technology is limited only by the human mind and by the availability of materials that can be devoted to the activity of education. The instructional reach of such an institution is limited only by the confines of the planet we live on. Indeed, in its ability to simultaneously teach large numbers of students in widespread locations, the on line university bears in it the seeds of a more integrated global society, a quality that might prove to be essential for the survival of humanity in the next century. Introduction on a global level makes it more likely that society will be able to cope with the awesome tasks of survival that confronts it, next year, next decade, next century. Seen from that perspective, the university of the future is not the last step in the development of education, but the next.

Stanley Warren is a principal academic computing consultant for Systems and Computer Technology Corporation, and has developed instructional support programs using computers in both a community college and a four-year institution. He also taught courses in the humanities, in literature and writing, and in data processing.

Telecommunications has tremendous potential for strengthening and revitalizing higher education. To accomplish this revitalization, new approaches to managing telecommunication activities may be necessary.

The Role and Management of Telecommunications in Higher Education

Alan Creutz

"It was the best of times; it was the worst of times." Charles Dickens's description of the period of the French Revolution also aptly describes the climate in higher education telecommunications today. Telecommunications, data communications, or computer networking, whatever term one chooses, is reshaping delivery, support, and administrative processes of higher education. While this has made possible great benefits, it has also introduced a number of serious management and cost issues institutions cannot afford to ignore.

Until recently, telecommunications was little more than a fancy word for telephones. Telecommunications was a fairly minor facilities management function; senior administrators rarely concerned themselves with it. The issues of data communications or information transfer were relegated to the province of the data processing department—which also produced the reams of green-bar paper reports and provided terminals for engineering students.

This chapter discusses the changing telecommunications environment and its implications for the managers of higher education institutions. Using examples of the ways in which advances in telecommunications

E. M. Staman (ed.). *Managing Information in Higher Education.*
New Directions for Institutional Research, no. 55. San Francisco: Jossey-Bass, Summer 1987.

technology have altered traditional patterns in the areas of student regulation, the educational process, and research, ways in which the new telecommunications can help colleges and universities carry out their mission more effectively are discussed, and the crucial management issues involved in realizing maximum benefit from telecommunications: technical leadership, centralization of the management function, performance and cost monitoring, planning, and institutional commitment are explored. The potential of telecommunications to strengthen and revitalize higher education is great, but careful planning and management are required to control costs and achieve optimum performance.

Impact on Registration

Times have certainly changed, as even a casual observer of the campus scene can attest. The dramatic changes wrought by the introduction of advanced telecommunications technology are exemplified by what has happened to the process of student registration at college. Twenty years ago, registration of students was done in what was known as the bull pen, where administrative staff sat at tables, each table equipped with just a few class sign-up sheets. Students waited in line for hours at each table. If they moved to the head of the line before the class they wanted was filled, they were registered. But when they went to another line and waited again to enroll for their next class, they were usually out of luck if that class was especially popular.

In the mid 1970s, on line student registration was introduced at many universities. Automatic scheduling of registration appointments and powerful programs permitting the terminal operator to resolve many problems of class conflicts and special prerequisites reduced the average time spent in registration from a full day to less than an hour. Students had better control over their schedules, and deans could make immediate decisions to add classes or rearrange schedules based on actual on line data.

Now, due to telecommunications, colleges in the 1980s have been able to move registration from administrative centers to dorms, libraries, and cafeterias. The new communications technology allows students to receive counseling and register for courses on terminals located throughout the campus. These on line student-counseling systems reduce the pressure on counselors and let the majority of students develop schedules at their leisure.

In the avant-garde of high-tech student registration, several colleges are now experimenting with new systems that will allow students to register from off-campus, without using computer terminals. Push-button telephones connect to computers with voice synthesizers. By pushing buttons on command, students can go through the entire registration process at home eliminating the trip to campus, lines, searching for trained computer operators, and the need to interact even with a standard computer terminal. In a business climate where eliminating obstacles to student enrollment is a key part of survival—especially in the community and vocational schools—telecommunications offer vital immediacy in the exchange of information.

Impact on the Educational Process

The use of telecommunications in higher education is not limited to the administration of the institution, however. The educational process itself is undergoing rapid changes to keep pace with technology. The rise of minicomputers and microcomputers, together with advances in data communications, has made large mainframe computers obsolete for most research purposes. Instead, computing resources are a mix of micrcomputers, usually networked with one or two minicomputers, and the sophisticated computing provided by major research centers located off-campus. Telecommunications technology has made this possible.

New supercomputers at a few major universities will soon deliver computing power through timesharing to colleges and universities throughout the United States. These computers supply the enormous data processing capacity required for large-scale modeling and data reduction activities. Managers of the new campus supercomputers have discovered major costs and problems associated with developing adequate telecommunications access to accommodate the demand for these computer resources, as users exchange information and access data bases on their colleagues' systems across campus, across the United States, and even internationally. With the growing accessibility of these powerful machines—just a telephone call away—local university mainframes are declining in importance, inefficient for large-scale, complex analyses and too expensive for the bulk of academic computing. Microcomputers and minicomputers—networked by sophisticated telecommunications—have become the mainstay of research computing.

To fully understand the impact of telecommunications and information technology on the instructional side of the house, we must understand the growing importance of computing in the educational process. New self-teaching techniques, changing student skills and academic expectations, and the vocational needs of students are forcing colleges to emphasize computing and student access to data communications networks as never before.

Engineering schools such as the New Jersey Institute of Technology, business schools such as Bentley College, and "megaversities" such as the Virginia Polytechnic Institute, all require freshmen to have networked microcomputers from the first day of class. The University of Pittsburgh is investing tens of millions of dollars in its "campus of the future." Sixty buildings on the central campus and four remote campuses will be linked by more than 11,000 communication lines of supporting voice, data, and video transmission. This network, involving microwave transmission, twisted-pair and coaxial cables, and fiber optics, employs virtually every telecommunications technology available today. It will provide access to the University's library catalogue, support automatic energy management, support omnipresent office automation, and include a computer connection in every dorm room. Similarly, Temple University in Philadelphia is nearing completion of a $12 million telecommunications network with private switches, microwave transmission, and fiber optics. The University of Michigan's network is just one telecommunications network among many now linking universities and research institutions throughout the world.

An Investment in Student Retention

At one prestigious liberal college in the Northeast, the president and the board of governors were deeply concerned that the quality of students was declining because the college was perceived as lacking an effective computing program and adequate support for student computer use. The board wondered if the image of the institution would improve if a requirement was made for every student to purchase a computer. Faculty members in the humanities were arguing that the college should spend millions of dollars to wire the dormitories—all built in the nineteenth century—so that students with computers would have access to networks and other campus computing resources. In fact, the college was debating wiring the dorms for computers while it still lacked telephones in the rooms!

Why are higher education institutions investing millions of dollars in telecommunications? There is at least one answer: survival. One of the most significant and obvious problems in higher education over the last few years has been the steady decline in college enrollments. Some Northeastern liberal arts colleges find applications have decreased more the 50 percent. On the other end of the spectrum, California community colleges have experienced actual declines in the student population of 25 percent and more. The Los Angeles Community College District has lost over 50,000 students in just three years. After the exciting times of the 1960s—exciting not only because of the political activism of the baby-boom generation but also because of new opportunities for growth and experimental course offerings—academic leaders of the 1970s and 1980s have had to face the fiscal reality of a dwindling market as the baby-boom generation has aged.

The decline in enrollments and the concomitant decrease in public funds have hurt every public school in the country. Private colleges have found they have only a limited ability to recoup costs by raising tuition fees. At the same time, daily operating expenses for educational institutions are increasing, due to increases in energy costs, unionization, increases in insurance premiums, and several other uncontrollable factors. In an age where competition is fierce, colleges and universities must provide state-of-the-art services to their students. Like industry, higher education must remain on the cutting edge of operational excellence. This means institutions must have the best facilities to attract the best faculty. And they must provide an information environment that prepares students to excel professionally in the next century. As companies like IBM and Digital Equipment Corporation—noted for their commitment to excellence—learned years ago, graduates from schools with the highest academic standards set America's management and business patterns. These students clearly recognize the vital role information technology—computing and telecommunications—will play in their individual success.

Financial Impact of Telecommunications Decisions

Telecommunications decisions are not trivial—we are talking about major expenditures. The average college in the United States spends between one-half and one percent of its total budget on telecommunications. This cost generally provides only basic service, support telephones and computer terminals. The scope of services needed will increase dramatically over the next five years. For example, office automation will swell the volume of data exchanged and the number of access points. The growing use of graphics will expand the volume of data in each transaction and the rise of video and image transfer threatens to increase data transfer requirements even more. These foreseeable factors alone will result in a dramatic leap in capacity requirements.

Telecommunications is expensive. A higher-education institution can easily spend one percent of its total budget on telecommunications—this can amount to millions of dollars in the larger universities. But deregulation has opened the door for a very interesting possibility for financing the institution's telecommunications bill. There are new opportunities to plug into national networks, to take advantage of consortia developing television courses, and to have greater accessibility to sister institutions locally and nationally.

Colleges and universities that provide dormitory housing for students or staff can now provide telecommunications services for their residents. Simply put, it means that the university can become the telephone company for the people living in university housing. Obviously there is extra cost in wiring the dormitories and providing services, but fees charged to students can help pay off both the incremental additional costs and some of the initial capital outlay for campus switches and systems.

Knowledge of telecommunications needs and plans should pervade all aspects of the institution's operations. For instance, no building renovation project should proceed without a thorough review of telecommunications capabilities and plans. When buildings are being remodeled, for example, options such as integrating voice, video, and image data should be considered. Security systems, fire detection systems, and energy management systems are all part of the telecommunications activities. Consider creating "smart buildings," which come equipped with cabling for all telecommunications functions.

It is probably not unreasonable to project that the telecommunications requirements in our colleges and universities will increase fivefold in the next ten years. Fortunately, this does not mean telecommunications costs also will increase fivefold.

The telecommunications function should have high visibility. It is a major expense, and will continue to change dramatically over the next few years. Important decisions will be made, whether through conscious deliberation or through inaction. Priorities for telecommunications should be a function of institutional needs, not local ambitions. The decisions will affect the fundamental way the institution administers itself, even permeating the educational process. Previously, institutions had little control over the costs of telephone systems, and the costs of data communications were not substantial. Institutional decisions made now on functionality, systems, and vendors can result in savings of millions of dollars over a few years. If these decisions are left to low-echelon managers, often with little technical expertise, the college runs a serious operational risk.

Consultants to the *Fortune* 1000 companies maintain that the average American business today spends nearly twice as much on telecommunications as it needs to. How can a college or university tell if it has achieved an appropriate balance between the resources invested in telecommunications and the quality of services received? The first warning signal is a telecommunications system that does not meet the college's needs: It cannot be expanded to add additional users, it cannot support required functions, or poor telecommunications support stymies plans to expand functions. These problems may be very concrete: No additional trunks are available in the Science Building; the cost of a microcomputer lab is excessive because of the cabling costs for the local area network; users complain of extended down time and maintenance complains of high maintenance costs; response times may be excessive, dial tones may be slow, and circuits noisy; or too often callers from the outside get busy signals or cannot reliably get messages to faculty members because telephones ring in empty offices or at nonresponsive message centers.

Conversely, the college may have an excess of resources. While lack of capacity and resources is usually obvious because users complain, excessive capacity is often invisible. Nevertheless, it is costly. If there are distinct telephone and data networks, there may well be idle capacity that could be used more efficiently. Are there enough WATS lines to handle all the calls made at 1:00 p.m. when administrators return to their offices and all decide simultaneously to call their colleagues across the country? Perhaps this excess capacity was purchased in anticipation of future growth. The danger is that by the time the need materializes, the technology will have evolved or needs will have changed.

Surprisingly, even with relatively simple telecommunications systems, there may be significant hidden costs from underused resources. Telephone circuit installation costs may come from departmental budgets rather than the central telecommunications budget. Local area networks and data communications for departmental computers rarely show up as a telecommunications cost, and personnel costs for supporting data networks may be buried in departmental budgets and the budget for computer services. Cabling is probably done by the plant operations group, in which case equipment may be procured from operating funds or even supplies budgets.

Telecommunications Management Issues

There is no question that telecommunications can help colleges and universities manage their operations more effectively, and offer better services and a better educational experience to their students. At the same time, telecommunications has opened a Pandora's box of management issues. As examples, colleges must decide whether to "go it alone" with private switches or use a public service provider like Centrex; whether to recable now or to wait for new advances in twisted-pair wiring for high-speed communications; and given a decision to move forward, choices such as fiber optics, TI lines, PBXs (Private Branch Exchanges), satellites, microwave communications, and so on must be made.

The number of vendors in the telecommunications field has mushroomed since deregulation. Full-service vendors provide both information systems and telecommunications, neatly bundled. However, there are also special service vendors, value-added consultants, and vendors with specialized products. Therefore, choosing vendors carefully is critical in high-tech areas, and the choices are not easy. Decisions about technology are complex and often emotionally charged, and the technology of telecommunications is more complex and more esoteric than that of microcomputing. The telecommunications manager has the added problem that today's layperson is more aware of high tech than ever before in history. A few hard-sell ads from a *Fortune* 1000 telecommunications company on fiber optics and the wonders it represents can lead a college president to conclude fiber optics will solve his institution's telecommunications needs. Generally, except in areas dedicated to research and development, educational institutions should not be experimenters in technology. Yet often the space-age appeal of the new technologies, combined with an institution's self-image as an innovator and leader, lead to daring experiments.

IBM's recent moves in networking provide insight into some of the problems involved in trying to manage telecommunications in a university setting. First IBM announced a Cabling System which, although incompatible with its own products, represented the backbone of IBM's future product strategy. This coaxial system met technical specifications different from those used either in existing IBM coaxial-based products or in common third-party systems. Then IBM announced the PC-Network, its flagship local area network, a broadband system using coaxial cable but not compatible with the IBM Cabling System. And most recently the company has announced a token-ring network as the new product of choice. IBM's inconsistency intensifies the confusion faced by colleges in plotting their telecommunications future.

As telecommunications technology advances, colleges and universities may need an on-campus expert or group that keeps informed and is able to make technical judgments. Telecommunications for an institution must be viewed as a global, strategic issue. Dealing with vendors, for instance, is becoming increasingly complicated—not only because of the multitude of vendors, but also because the systems offered are more complex. Multi-vendor environments are increasingly common, and with them comes the requirement for more expertise in understanding how different products relate and how to establish performance criteria. A principal manager can understand the entire telecommunications system for the entire institution and can make the most intelligent decisions about specific applications for specific users. A manager of telecommunications should be a senior person within the institution, on a level with the manager of information systems, reporting to a vice-president. During the start-up phase, particularly if the institution expects to make a heavy capital investment, this manager might even report directly to the president. The key to the reporting relationship is to ensure that telecommunications receives the visibility and support it needs from senior management.

Although a telecommunications manager must thoroughly understand telecommunications technology, she or he must be far more than a technician. The manager must serve as part of the institutional planning team, being involved in making and implementing college policy. There are very few trained telecommunications managers available—hence the job often falls to the manager of information systems. This will work, as long as information systems personnel recognize that telecommunications is more than data communications and give it the attention and priority it deserves. Even if the same person serves as manager of the telecommunications and the information systems departments in the role of chief information officer, the two functions should remain distinct.

Historically, data networks have been the province of data processing management and all other telecommunications has been handled by a separate office. As access to computing becomes more widespread, and as the technologies supporting data communications and other telecommunications converge, the distinction between management information systems and telecommunications is rapidly disappearing. There is now a "spectrum of technology." Where, for instance, does electronic mail fit into the traditional organizational structure? Electronic mail often is implemented on a mainframe or minicomputer—traditional data processing services—although it functionally resembles telecommunications more than computing. Increasingly, computing networks and telephones share facilities; the PBX is actually a computer.

As telecommunications becomes more complex and its scope expands, the management of telecommunications comes to resemble the management of information systems. However, it is often not necessary or organizationally appropriate to merge the two management functions. Nevertheless, the interdependence of the two requires increasingly close coordination. The integrated management team must support traditional data processing, telephones, electronic mail, office automation, video and image processing, and decision support. Each manager must understand the other's technology. For example, the use of communications lines for data exchange is different from the use of those same lines for voice. A telecommunications manager must not only understand data communications but, in today's sophisticated environment, probably manage several computers.

Advantages of Centralization

An ideal telecommunications department is centralized. All telecommunications issues should be handled in one office, and include planning, engineering, performance, operations, maintenance, and procurement for both telephones and data communications. In addition, the organization has top-level visibility, ideally with a direct reporting relationship to senior institutional management. The telecommunications office must not only handle the day-to-day mechanics of running systems switches and networks, it must also provide a support structure for the entire institution's communications purchases.

In a well-managed telecommunications function, a central office handles vendor relations and issues. Properly made, a telecommunications procurement decision involves evaluating the need, identifying all suitable products, developing selection criteria, performing a financial analysis of return-on-investment, preparing a bid request, evaluating vendors and their ability to service the equipment, and supervising installation. These are not tasks for amateurs, no matter how well informed they may be. Even if professionals within user departments perform these activities, decisions cannot be made in isolation. New systems must be compatible with existing systems, and management should be alert for ways to share resources. Decentralized management can lead to duplication and costly attempts to interface products with different technologies from different vendors.

A telecommunications department should handle all maintenance, operations, and engineering for telecommunications. In this capacity, it should provide technical support for all telecommunications, including preparing specifications and configurations, managing acquisitions and systems implementation, and providing operational support and maintenance. In addition, it should provide regular reports to users on performance and administrative reports as they are needed for planning, cost evaluation, and chargebacks and budgeting. Ongoing long-range planning processes will help ensure that telecommunications services meet future needs. Regular cost-benefit evaluations, technology assessments, futures planning to anticipate new needs and products, and regularly updated capacity plans are the essential elements.

The department should have mechanisms for monitoring performance and costs of telecommunications and for reporting relevant information to user departments and to senior management. Telecommunications is no different from any other business function: Without good controls there is no way of evaluating effectiveness and improving efficiency.

Most important, the telecommunications department must be prepared to work effectively with users to resolve problems, prepare feasibility studies for enhancements and new applications, and assist the other department managers in all phases of planning and operation. The best control mechanisms and management structures in the world can be rendered ineffective by a lack of cooperation. Good communication and rapport will be especially critical with information systems personnel, both administrative and academic. Nothing will more quickly vitiate the effectiveness of the telecommunications department than frustration among the instructors and researchers using computer resources resulting from nonresponsive attitudes on the part of informations systems personnel. Of course, poor cooperation often derives from territorial disputes between computing and telecommunications people.

Pointing out the possible problems with current telecommunications management is one thing. It is quite another to identify solutions. Institutional preferences for centralized-versus-decentralized operation, existing organizational structures, size, magnitude, and types of telecommunications requirements are all major factors in developing an appropriate telecommunications function. It would be an oversimplification to suggest there is one ideal answer to fit every college and university. But there are guidelines for defining specific solutions.

As with computing, it is important to establish fundamental criteria to be used in evaluating a technology, a project, or a system. No matter how appealing a technical solution may be, it should not be implemented unless it serves the functional needs of the institution. Every purchase of telecommunications equipment and service, and every decision that bears on telecommunications in any way, must be evaluated as a business decision. Reporting and planning processes must be followed to ensure a business approach. To this end, four criteria should be kept in mind:

- *Effectiveness:* Doing the right thing
- *Efficiency:* Doing the thing right
- *Volume:* Getting the most out with the least in
- *Value:* Progress toward objectives.

For telecommunications to be effective, efficient, and valuable, the institution must have a coherent investment policy based on careful analysis of needs and adequate planning, building upon institutional strategic plans, clear priorities, and effective coordination. Adherence to these criteria will establish the baseline for a sound telecommunications organization and a sound management information systems organizations.

Telecommunications Business Plans

In the corporate world, any operational function as important as telecommunications would advisedly be guided by a formal business plan. This plan indicates the basic goals and objectives to be achieved, the strategy to be followed, the organization, the resources required (and revenues generated), and the criteria to be used to evaluate effectiveness. The importance of business planning for telecommunications in higher education is at least equal to other planning activities: computing, curricula, marketing, and so on.

Several overriding issues should be included in the telecommunications business plan. First, progress in telecommunications cannot be accomplished without first establishing an institutional commitment to effective telecommunications involving senior management. One possible way to develop an effective institutional commitment is to establish a telecommunications task force consisting of senior deans and chaired by the vice-president of information systems or the vice-president of administration. Perhaps another vice-president or two should also be involved. This task force should include technical experts and representatives of user groups. The committee should be constituted in such a way that the members have some technical savvy but are not committed to technology already in place. The mission is to meet current and projected needs, not to continue current practices.

Another way to achieve an institutional commitment is to hire a consultant (who reports to the president or a senior vice-president) to review the institution's telecommunications needs and systems. Many institutions feel that the objectivity of an outsider is worth the investment. If there is already an experienced telecommunications expert within the organization with a broad view of institutional operations, he or she can represent the focal point for the process.

In any event, an institution wide review of telecommunications may well encounter resistance. If several local telecommunications projects are already in place—local minicomputer systems and local area networks, perhaps even a telephone switch—their managers will probably be strongly committed to these operations. An institutional review of telecommunications may be perceived as a threat, both by those whose operations have been working effectively and by those who have developed inefficient management empires. However, strong and supportive senior management involvement can simultaneously highlight the importance and ultimate benefits of this review process and ease understandable tensions among incumbent telecommunications personnel.

The objectives of this review are to identify all telecommunications functions, to evaluate costs and performance, effectiveness, staffing, and so on, and to develop a comprehensive plan for future expansion and capital expenditures. The first step in such a review is to make an inventory of all existing telecommunications activities and systems, even those not supported by advanced technology. This will involve reviewing telephone call records and bills, data networks, communications traffic volume, performance reports, work time reported in support of telecommunications, and so on. Even if the institution currently uses Centrex, a surprising amount of data can be collected and analyzed from telephone company data tapes, which detail each call made.

The institution's entire communications structure must be reviewed. A realistic and accurate assessment includes not only electronic telecommunications but communications of all types. Indeed, areas may be discovered that lack electronic communications and that ought to be supported by technology. All offices that physically exchange data by diskette or paper must be evaluated as part of the communications review. As part of this review process, the task force should look for redundant communication networks where multiple circuits run along parallel paths or where two or more systems provide similar or identical services. They should also identify any idle or underused resources: telephone lines or computers that are operating well below capacity for no apparent reason. The review should examine old technologies that might be candidates for enhancement or upgrade to ensure the institution is getting the best performance for its dollar.

The total expenditure for telecommunications must be established, including dollars spent in specific areas that users may be reluctant to acknowledge. That physics lab with the sophisticated local network cannot be ignored any more than the bookstore computing system or the automated library network. Accurate evaluations for cost and benefits cannot be made without complete information. After completing the review of current activities, systems, and needs, the task force should reassess them in terms of current technology. Care must be taken in this review not to be carried away with the glamour of the new technology. Except in a specific research context, higher educational institutions typically cannot afford to be in the forefront of technological experimentation.

After performance of these inventories and assessments, the task force, consultant, or designated telecommunications manager, working with telecommunications experts, must cooperate with the institutional strategic planning team. Effective telecommunications planning, like information systems planning, cannot occur independently of strategic planning. It is not uncommon to discover during a review of institutional needs for information systems and telecommunications that the institutional strategic plan is inadequate. The role of computing in delivery of instruction, especially, is often ill-defined, although that role has profound impact on both information systems planning and costs, and on telecommunications activities. If the college plans a widespread, integrated office automation environment with powerful decision support systems paralleling those in the commercial sector, it must prepare for it in the telecommunications plan.

Short-Term Telecommunications Planning

A good technique for getting the telecommunications function organized is to develop a short-term telecommunications improvement or stabilization plan. Concurrently, determine an interim organization for the telecommunications function, selecting the individuals to be assigned to it and the reporting structure. This may require adding new personnel if feasible, or reassigning personnel. If the institution lacks qualified technical personnel, it is especially important to get started quickly because finding or training qualified technical people is a long process.

The short-term plan should focus on service problems. Specific problems within the organization may include inadequate service to users and high costs that can be quickly reduced. A good inventory of current activities should reveal operational concerns, such as excessive down-time or inadequate capacity. Addressing these concerns, while reducing costs, gains quick credibility for the project. Usually, a combination of effective, active management coupled with senior-level commitment can make significant progress in six months, thereby convincing doubters of the worth of the evaluation process to the institution in the near and long term.

To establish this credibility, it is important during the first months to identify goals that can be met. Keep commitments within reason, clearly identify the goals to be met, and publicize the successes. A core task of this short-term telecommunications improvement program is to develop a long-term plan. This plan should address goals and objectives, priorities, organization, time lines, strategies, and resource requirements. The short-term program should be a model for the ongoing improvement activity. Hence, success in the short-term plan will be the best groundwork for long-term success; but problems in the short term could mean problems in the long term.

Once the short-term plan is in place, the task force or responsible senior manager should prepare recommendations for establishing a long-term management organization for telecommunications. Because the long-term management structure must fit both the institutional culture and ensure high user confidence, good rapport must be established with all user areas. The long-term management structure for telecommunications should reflect strong central control or support substantial departmental autonomy as appropriate within the institutional culture. However, the decision process for telecommunications should reside in a single group with the requisite resources, authority, and expertise.

Summary

The issues and the technology of telecommunications are complex and exciting. The benefits are clear. Whether institutional management is ready or not, faculty and students are demanding sophisticated telecommunications structures in our colleges and universities. In administration, research, and teaching, new activities and methods require increasingly powerful and widespread telecommunications support.

Accommodating these demands for advanced telecommunications technology requires institutional commitment and dedicated management to contain costs and achieve optimal performance. Telecommunications is integral to the mission of higher education; management of telecommunications must be integral to the institution's organizational structure. Colleges and universities should centralize the management of telecommunications and appoint a telecommunications manager who can provide the forward-looking technical leadership needed to realize the benefits of new technologies. Centralization provides maximum efficiency in acquisition, selection, monitoring, and maintenance of equipment; reduces costs; and permits effective long-range planning. Centralized management, however, does not imply central control. In fact, the most effective telecommunications managers are those who can lead their institutions.

Telecommunications has become a major phenomenon in higher education, one that cannot be ignored. Its potential to revitalize and strengthen the institution is great, but senior-level, centralized management is required if this potential is to be realized in a cost-effective manner.

Alan Creutz, a systems consultant with Management Analysis Company in San Diego, California, has been involved in higher education since 1972 as a faculty member, administrator, and most recently as a consultant. His work has stressed the intimate relationship of telecommunications and information systems, and the need for enlightened management that guides, rather than constricts, those systems.

Awareness of the advantages and limitations inherent in applying different tools in different environments is essential to their appropriate and optimal applications.

Using Fourth-Generation Tools in Information Management

R. Gregory Litaker

With increasing frequency, data processing managers are considering fourth-generation languages to be effective solutions to the applications backlog problem. These products, which have most often been used as productivity aids for mainframe applications programmers, have generally produced a positive return on the investment required for their acquisition and start up. The recent emergence of fourth-generation software for microcomputers, and end-users who want to use this software to develop production applications, presents yet another situation for which the data center manager needs to perform a cost-benefit assessment.

Driven by a growing applications backlog and a user community that wants more direct control of information resources, institutions are moving quickly to employ fourth-generation technology to improve the productivity in the applications development cycle. With the acquisition and use of these products, colleges are entering a new era in the management of information systems development.

Applications will now be developed employing three distinct types of programming personnel. Traditional applications programmers, information center specialists and end-users, will be individually or coopera-

E. M. Staman (ed.). *Managing Information in Higher Education.*
New Directions for Institutional Research, no. 55. San Francisco: Jossey-Bass, Summer 1987.

tively responsible for developing the information systems that will be used for reporting research and decision support in the future. This chapter describes the promises and pitfalls of this expanding development environment.

Fourth-Generation Tools

There is currently no consensus as to what constitutes a fourth-generation development tool. However, for the present discussion certain characteristics will be accepted as lending fourth-generation quality to a product (Glover, 1984; Goetz, 1982; Martin, 1982):

- An integral data dictionary exists
- The data base can be created and modified easily
- Users view data as relational tables of columns and rows
- Interactive retrieval and reporting facilities are available
- Significantly less coding is required to accomplish the same task as would be required using a high-level language such as COBOL
- The user can tell the computer what needs to be done without specifying how to do it.

The last characteristic, while simplistic, summarizes the essential element that allows nonprogrammers to use these new tools to develop their own applications.

Some mainframe products that have one or more of these characteristics and that are available on many campuses are "EASYTRIEVE" and "EASYTRIEVE PLUS" by Pansophic, Statistical Analysis System ("SAS") by SAS Institute, "FOCUS" by Information Builders, "ORACLE" by Oracle Corp., and "MANTIS" by Cincom. Similarly, microcomputer products such as "dBase" by Ashton-Tate and "Lotus 1-2-3" by Lotus Development, which are readily available, are endowed with many of the fourth-generation qualities described above.

Expanding Applications Development Environment

Several computing industry trends are combining to create conditions where the applications development process can be undertaken by persons not trained as programmers. End-users are rapidly becoming more literate in computing because of increased availability of microcomputers and are becoming more involved in computing activities (Martin, 1982; and Goetz, 1982). Additionally, the industry is producing more sophisticated productivity tools that can be used by both professional and novice users to quickly develop a variety of applications.

At most colleges and universities these trends have manifested themselves in predictable ways. In the user community there is an increasing dependency on microcomputing and a growing need for a micro-main-frame link. Users are involved in the use of batch report writers and desire a similar tool for on line access to the university data bases. In the data center there is a need for productivity tools, a better way to support ad hoc reporting requirements, and a more productive way to respond to the growing applications backlog.

In an effort to capitalize on these trends and to assess the viability of using fourth-generation tools for applications development, some institutions have created a service unit called the "information center" (Moskovis, Staman, and Litaker, 1983; Hamilton, 1986; and Matross, 1986). Two primary goals of these centers are to: (1) provide users with the tools to access and explore their data in their own way, and (2) provide efficient response to ad hoc user requests for reports and information.

The information center embodies the concept of the expanding applications development environment (LaPlante, 1986). It is staffed by information specialists (nonprogrammers) to assist end-users (nonprogrammers) in developing their own applications.

The sections that follow discuss how various fourth-generation productivity tools can be introduced and applied by a regular programming staff, information center specialists, and end-users. A case study is then presented to describe one university's experience with fourth-generation tools.

Impact on Different Developmental Environments

One of the clearest results of the use of fourth-generation tools havs been a fundamental change in the applications development environment. The information centers and end-user computing are two environments that simply did not exist at any measurable level ten, or even five, years ago. The result of this evolution is that the definition of a computing user has changed to include those individuals who now can invoke any of a variety of fourth-generation tools on an ad hoc basis.

The following sections focus on the impact of fourth-generation tools on three developmental environments: the traditional environment, the information specialist's environment, and the end-user environment. In each case, the following areas are reviewed: nature of the users, required training, user acceptance of fourth-generation tools, utility of fourth-generation tools, and evaluation of a completed project.

Traditional Environment

For purposes of discussion in this chapter, computer users in the traditional development environment are applications programming staffs. Academic backgrounds are typically two- and four-year degrees; professional training backgrounds usually with emphasis on application languages, data base, and so on.

For this group, training in the use of a fourth-generation tool can usually be accomplished in one to five days, depending on the complexity of the product. In addition to basic training, key issues for the traditional group include evaluation of the appropriate use of each kind of applications development tool (optimizing on development effort, end-product quality, and machine resource utilization), and of which of the university's policies such as security, ownership, and privacy of data apply in a given situation.

Programmers usually view fourth-generation tools as productivity aids for parts of some applications. Ad hoc reporting, prototyping, and the development of relatively unsophisticated applications are examples. A typical design might involve limited user data entry, appropriate editing, noncomplex data manipulation, and relatively straightforward screens or reports. The use of the fourth-generation tools for applications meeting these criteria tend to have a relatively high degree of programmer acceptance.

Information Specialist's Environment

The information specialist can be described as an individual with responsibility for areas such as the user services function, user training, and user consulting. Academic backgrounds vary, and professional training need not include programming or formal education in information systems development. In fact, information specialists may more likely have formal training or experience in one or more areas of user expertise, for example the registrar's office, institutional research, budget analysis, and admissions. Computing experience is usually developed as a natural by-product of activity as computing users.

The development environment in this case might well be under the egis of an information center. For this group of individuals, in addition to the basic skills required to use the available fourth-generation tools, training must include strong emphasis on the design and functions of existing university information systems. In addition, training should include the appropriate policy and procedural issues and some information about how to train users. These individuals will become the primary trainers for the user community.

Although the classical approach to an information center would suggest that applications are developed by end-users instead of information specialists, clearly these latter individuals have become users in their own right. In addition to training and consulting activities, however, information center staffs can become involved in ad hoc programming, probably out of necessity rather than as a result of a mission definition. In the information center developmental environment, then, fourth-generation tools have a high degree of support and strong staff advocacy. This is due to both the nature of the center's mission and because fourth-generation tools are one of the primary agents for the center to accomplish its mission.

The information specialists have had the broadest exposure to fourth-generation tools. It is from this group that data processing departments may ultimately derive the most productivity from these tools. Unlike programmers, this group can usually gain higher levels of proficiency with these tools because they use them on a regular basis and train end-users to make use of them.

End-User Environment

This aspect of the discussion will focus on those users who are not members of either computing center staffs or of information center staffs. They are, in fact, the primary audience for which fourth-generation tools are actually intended: people with little or no background in computing who want to use computers in their work.

Training is conducted by a number of groups, including information specialists, data center employees, and vendors. Training, which is typically limited to the use of a given product, is often at a somewhat abstract level of description of a product's features and how they work. The training should more appropriately be application-oriented and should therefore include strong components of all applications systems in a given user area. The intent should be not only to develop expertise in the use of a given tool, but also to develop "better" users—those able to participate more fully in the planning and direction of the university's large-scale, centralized information systems (Denise, 1983).

In the same sense that few are more enthusiastic about a new product than the product's developers, end-users who successfully apply a fourth-generation tool to a problem in their area typically become among the strongest advocates of the tool. As such, their experience presents opportunities upon which to expand the development of end-user computing. Techniques include user office demonstrations, consulting, and return-on-investment arguments—all of which are effective methods to strengthen the base upon which the end-user community is building. As a result, the natural tendency for the users to be highly supportive and positive about fourth-generation tools will continue to be reinforced.

A Case Study

Prompted by an increasing backlog of requested applications, Western Michigan University (WMU) made a decision to encourage the use of fourth-generation technologies for applications development. It was further decided that since fourth-generation tools were purported to be "friendly" enough for a variety of user skill levels, several new development environments would be evaluated as alternatives to the central data processing development scheme. WMU employed three unique groups of applications developers working individually or cooperatively to create several significant applications. The development groups were: data processing applications programmers, information specialists from WMU's information center, and several end-users from administrative offices.

Fourth-generation tools available to WMU personnel included report writers "EASYTRIEVE" and "EASYTRIEVE PLUS," Statistical Analysis System ("SAS"), and "MANTIS," a data base programming language. Microcomputer products that were used in this evaluation were "dBase" II and III data base programming languages, and "Multiplan" and "Lotus 1-2-3" spreadsheet products.

Traditional Development. Shortly after WMU acquired "MANTIS," a senior programmer was assigned the task of using the product to develop an on line data entry application that would interface with an existing inventory system. The project involved creating and integrating several functional screens that allowed menu selection of activity, data entry, data editing, query, and browse capabilities. Additionally, all of these transactions used Cincom's "TOTAL" as the data base. The project resulted in a useful system that has become a vital part of the inventory operation at WMU.

The project was not without its flaws, however. The complexity of the task and unfamiliarity with "MANTIS" caused frustrating delays while features and capabilities were explored. An extended learning period with less ambitious projects would have improved programmer satisfaction.

Information Center Consultant. At WMU, consulting support for "EASYTRIEVE" applications has been available from the office of Data Processing for many years. This service has produced individuals with a high degree of skill in using this product to satisfy ongoing or ad hoc reporting requirements.

Recent additions of "SAS" and "MANTIS" have provided new tools for which proficiencies must be developed and appropriate uses found. Two projects exemplify how these products are being integrated into the available application development tools of the information specialist.

A data entry system for the Public Safety Division was written using "MANTIS." The application system was designed to collect parking violation ticket information on a daily basis. The system was menu-controlled and provided capabilities for entry, editing, search, and retrieval of parking ticket information. The initial "MANTIS" learning curve for the developer of this application was expectedly slower than for a programmer. But techniques learned early in the development were easily recalled and used later in the process.

This application has now been scheduled for production implementation. Because of the ability to "prototype" the application for the end-user and to interactively build and modify screens during the development process, users are expected to have a high degree of satisfaction upon implementation.

The specialist who developed this application noted none of the concerns about the process expressed by the programming group. The most serious difficulty encountered was with file interfacing and a lack of knowledge about the "TOTAL" data base. The overall reaction to this experience was very positive. There was strong acceptance of the product and anticipation that it would be a useful tool for assisting end-users in developing other applications.

"SAS" was first used and introduced to the administrative end-user community when an ad hoc report request was presented by the personnel department. Typically, this type of request would have been an "EASY-TRIEVE" application, but in an effort to use and expose new tools and services to the users, "SAS" was selected for the project.

User reaction indicates that the ease of using "SAS" commands for producing formatted list reports and graphic data representations may quickly make it the language of choice over "EASYTRIEVE" for certain types of ad hoc requests. Additionally, "SAS" may prove to be a more palatable product and encourage end-users to develop their own applications.

End-User Development. While end-users have had access to "EASY-TRIEVE" for many years, perhaps the most productive use of fourth-generation products is coming from the newer microcomputer-based products. Several examples will serve to illustrate this trend and its potential impact on data processing.

"Multiplan" has become the staple spreadsheet software for financial administrative applications on microcomputers. In some cases, data that have been compiled through the use of "EASYTRIEVE" reports are subsequently loaded to a "Multiplan" spreadsheet. Using the same skeletal shell month after month eliminates the need for proofreading, footing, and ticking. The next logical step will be to directly link the data created by "EASYTRIEVE" to the already created "Multiplan" spreadsheet. Utility programs such as "LOADCALC" appear to possess the capability to bridge this gap. A project to test the feasibility of this concept is under consideration at the present time.

Some applications have been best handled completely through "Multiplan" with no interaction with the mainframe computer. An example of this is the Daily Cash Expense and Receipt report and the Cash Percentage report generated for WMU's Office of Investments and Risk Management. In this case, a very sophisticated application was developed for the investments office to reflect the daily impact of cash inflows, outflows, and investments. In addition, the various fund entities were calculated as a percentage of investment ownership on a daily rolling basis. This application is an example of optimal use of the data center specialist as a consultant. If this application had been attempted as a traditional mainframe project, the development time would have been longer, the user would have had a less flexible solution, and data processing would have had responsibility for maintaining the product.

From a user perspective, there are several benefits to a product such as "MANTIS." First, even when the product is used solely by a data center programmer or specialist, the end-user can get a preview of data entry screens before a significant amount of effort has been expended. This is especially important when systems are being refined on an ongoing basis. Second, the end-users can now request applications that would have required a substantial commitment of human resources if programmed through the traditional IBM "CICS" environment. A general ledger on line data entry system has been quickly developed by taking advantage of these capabilities.

At this time, only data center staff are using "MANTIS." However, as with "EASYTRIEVE," end-users will undoubtedly employ this tool to create inquiry and data entry screens in the future.

The "dBase" product has provided users an alternative method for developing certain limited application systems. An example of this is WMU's Department of Public Safety (DPS). DPS has an application that collects tremendous volumes of detailed crime statistics data on a tape-based mainframe system with a low keypunch and processing priority. DPS staff independently developed several separate microcomputer data bases that contained the specific data for victims, crimes, suspects, and property. Although these applications taxed the limits of "dBase II," the introduction of "dBase III" will alleviate such problems. In any case, this application demonstrates an appropriate balance between micro and main-frame. DPS staff now have control over immediate data entry and file updating. This gives them a significant advantage in producing their detailed weekly reports, which are printed directly from the micro. How-ever, there is still a need for the capabilities of the mainframe processor. Monthly reports that involve indexing and sorting and then printing of the entire data bases involve much more processing capability and much faster printing capability than can be found at the micro level.

The solution, therefore, has been to send the appropriate data to the mainframe via an "IRMA" board from Digital Communications Asso-ciates, Inc., on the micro. Once the data are received by the mainframe, they can be sorted and printed for reports and sent to tape for state police statistical requirements. This application has accomplished two significant goals: first, it gives DPS better control and turnaround time, and second, it removes a substantial keypunch burden from the data entry staff in the data center.

A final example serves as a clear description of the possibilities afforded through the use of fourth-generation tools. The personnel office expressed a desire to develop a data base application on their personal computer. They were willing to invest their time in the development process but knew nothing about programming. After discussions with the information center staff to explore the complexity of the project, it was decided to test the use of one of the new application program generators (APG) for microcomputer-based products. An APG is a program that allows the user to design on the video screen the data entry, retrieval, and report formats for a system. The program then generates executable program modules that perform all the functions of data entry, edit, retrieval, and reporting.

With very little assistance the user from personnel was able to use "QuickCode III," a "dBase II" program development tool, to design a fully functional data entry and retrieval system that was built to his exact specifications.

User Experiences. Overall evaluations of fourth-generation products from the user perspective are very positive. Applications have been successfully addressed in virtually every case. However, from the user perspective, there remain areas of concern with regard to fourth-generation products.

Tools such as "MANTIS" and "FOCUS" will open many doors for users on an institutionwide basis. But care must be exercised so as not to jeopardize the control and integrity of system files and programs. Increased accessibility must be monitored and evaluated.

End-users should be encouraged in their use and appreciation of fourth-generation tools. However, there appears to be a danger that if left unattended, the user could easily wander off-track and become inefficient or ineffective in his or her use of such products. For this reason, it appears necessary for the staff of the data centers to closely monitor all use of such products.

Finally, even though there are many applications where the use of fourth-generation languages is appropriate, it is important that users learn and understand the proper use, limitations, and responsibilities that accompany their use (McKinney, Schott, Teeter, and Mannering, 1986).

Summary

Management of the fourth-generation experience is in many ways similar to any other product-acquisition project. First, an assessment must be made of the match between available products, organizational needs, and staff capabilities. Because some products are better as report writers, others as query tools, and still others for systems development, the needs of the organization should help clarify the type of product that will be most beneficial.

The professional level, competence, and availability of the staff who will use the product should be given appropriate consideration. For example, does the product have a sufficiently rich language and editor to support your programming staff? Are its features too complex for your user community? How much training is required and available in order to use the product to its best potential?

The technical features and capabilities of a desirable product may be related to your data processing environment. The abilities to interface with an existing data base or file structure, or to call external procedures from your applications library may be critical issues in your considerations. Additionally, if incorporating microcomputers into your systems plan is important, the selection of a product that either supports micro-mainframe interaction or has compatible micro and mainframe versions can present a useful solution.

Colleges are becoming increasingly committed to putting more computing services into the users' hands. To that end, the continued development of and dependence on fourth-generation products for applications development will continue to grow.

References

Denise, R. M. "Technology for the Executive Thinker." *Datamation*, 1983, *29* (6), 206–216.

Glover, R. "A Fourth-Generation Approach to Decision Support in a Private University." Paper represented at the 24th Annual Forum of the Association for Institutional Research, Fort Worth, Tex., May 6–9, 1984.

Goetz, M. "Engineering Fourth-Generation System Software." *Computerworld*, June 7, 1982, supp., pp. 1–14.

Hamilton, S. "Institutional Research and the Information Center: Two Functions or One?" Paper presented at the 26th Annual Forum of the Association for Institutional Research, Orlando, Fla., June 22–25, 1986.

LaPlante, A. "The Rise and Development of the Information Center." *InfoWorld*, 1986, *8* (35), 27–28.

McKinney, R., Schott, J., Teeter, D., and Mannering, L. "The Role of Institutional Research in Data Administration and Management." Paper presented at the 26th Annual Forum of the Association for Institutional Research, Orlando, Fla., June 22–25, 1986.

Martin, J. *Application Development Without Programmers.* Englewood Cliffs, N.J.: Prentice-Hall, 1982.

Matross, R. "Designing the Information Center: An Analysis of Markets and Delivery Systems." Paper presented at the 26th Annual Forum of the Association for Institutional Research, Orlando, Fla., June 22–25, 1986.

Moskovis, L., Staman, E. M., and Litaker, R. G. "The Information/Decision Support Center." Paper presented at CAUSE National Conference, San Francisco, December 11–14, 1983.

R. Gregory Litaker is a senior principal consultant with Systems and Computer Technology Corporation. His activities have included data center management, technical consulting, and the development of long range plans for information technology at several colleges and universities. Prior to joining SCT, Dr. Litaker served higher education for ten years in offices of institutional research and planning.

In a decentralized data environment, a critical need exists for effective, efficient, and appropriate administration of institutional data.

Data Administration and Management

Richard L. McKinney, John S. Schott, Deborah J. Teeter, Linda W. Mannering

Administrative use of the microcomputer has had a profound impact on college and university operations. In particular, administrative computing activities, once the sole responsibility of the central computing enterprise within an institution, are now widely dispersed throughout the organization. Powerful, easy-to-use desktop computers and user-friendly software have enabled professionals at virtually every operational level to participate in the collection, analysis, and reporting of data. As users request and acquire data, and become more proficient in manipulating those data, they assume a more active role in data-related operations. It is these expanding roles, new capabilities, and new expectations that have serious implications for effective data administration and management.

This chapter describes the computer-driven data and information needs of various organizational units and the transition to data administration. It focuses on several key issues surrounding the decentralization of data: data access, data integrity, data manipulation, data analysis and interpretation, and data reporting. Finally, the role of institutional research in the administration and management of data is discussed.

E. M. Staman (ed.). *Managing Information in Higher Education.*
New Directions for Institutional Research, no. 55. San Francisco: Jossey-Bass, Summer 1987.

Historic Roles

Administrative computing has been the traditional workhorse that develops and maintains the basic operating systems of an institution. The financial, personnel, student, and facilities operations systems often are included in administrative computing responsibilities. These systems support the ongoing processes of an organization.

Administrative operations such as personnel, accounting, and admissions and records are the primary users of administrative data that are designed to support their functions. Managers are concerned with the straightforward stocks and flows of the items for which they are responsible: personnel counts employees, the comptroller counts dollars, and admissions and records counts students.

Complementing these operations is institutional research, typically the principal analytical arm of the institution. The gathering, synthesizing, analyzing, and reporting of data to support decision making is a major institutional research function. Institutional researchers are heavy users of administrative data in their roles as data interpreter and information purveyor. Central and academic administrations are the principal recipients of operational and analytical data that provide information and insight about how an organization has performed (dollars spent, students enrolled), and suggest implications for the future based on data trends.

Emerging Roles

With the introduction of the microcomputer, the lines that delineated the roles of providers and recipients of information have been blurred. Today, almost anyone with a minimum of microcomputing competence can assume the role of data generator, analyzer, or reporter. Data from any source can be manipulated and adjusted to present an accurate picture. The explosive growth of data-related activities throughout higher education has driven home the realization that the days of casual use of data are gone forever. From the staff member in the smallest administrative department to the president of the institution, the "wild west" mentality of data use must become more civilized.

Bias is an all too common factor in the data and information business, and an effort to limit bias and contradictory reporting through effective data management and administration is an important and difficult task. It is important, however, not to confuse data management and administration with rigid control. Excessive data regulation may exceed legal boundaries and is inappropriate in an institution of higher education. It is vital to have an effective data administration and management function in place as organizations make the transition from centrally controlled and manipulated data to decentralized data. Plourde (1986) points out that "the proliferation of micros has reinforced the need for centralized control rather than eliminating it," and stresses that "standards are crucial if we are to maintain the institutional view of the computing resource" (p. 23).

Transition to Data Administration

As the data processing field grew, it was first believed that a data base administrator (DBA) using a data base management system (DBMS) would solve many of the technical, administrative, and procedural data processing problems. Specific problems included the collection, processing, integration, security, and dissemination of data. Initially it was envisioned that the DBA/DBMS combination would be the focal point for all matters concerning data. This proved not to be the case as the DBA became totally engulfed in the technical aspects of the DBMS, with little or no time for what is now considered data administration. Thus, in the mid 1970s, the role of data administrator emerged and began to assume the DBA's job of interfacing the DBMS with the application programmers, users, and executives (Barnett Data Systems, 1982b). The need and demand for effective data administration has been spurred by the growing and diverse number of end-users. Information centers, in the role of facilitating end-user requirements, have accelerated this need.

Data base administration involves the technical and mechanical aspects of electronic data processing. The major concerns of data base administration include:

- Mapping data elements into records, and the records into an appropriate data structure
- Establishing an effective strategy for the physical placement of data
- Selecting one or more access methods/reference paths through the data base
- Implementing procedures to provide the necessary level of data security, integrity, and recovery (Uhrbach, 1980).

Data administration, in contrast, focuses on the analytical and not the technical aspects of data. The overall goals of data administration are to facilitate:

- Access to an understanding, reliability, accuracy, completeness, consistency, and currency of systems documentation
- Systems planning, development, and maintenance
- Use of DBMS and other software products
- Coordination in all matters relative to data resources, their organization, and their effectiveness and control (Barnett Data Systems, 1982a).

Once again, the demand for decentralizing data has focused attention on the need to establish a data administration function to assure that users who obtain access to institutional data bases understand the content and anomalies of the data. A primary goal of data administration should be to enlighten users in order to minimize bias and contradictory reporting of data. Hoffmann (1986) cites David Libensen as believing that data administration is one of the most important, yet least understood, aspects of records management. From Libensen's perspective, data administration "is the method by which the knowledge base . . . is maintained" (p. 40).

Decentralizing Data:
The Need for Protecting the Information Resource

Plourde (1986) states that "our [data administrator's] role increasingly is to monitor, to audit, and to ensure that we are protecting the [institutional] information base" (p. 24). A decentralized data environment requires that an organization come to grips with a number of critical data issues. These issues include data access, integrity, manipulation, analysis and interpretation, and reporting. The purpose of this section is to discuss the importance of these issues to institutional research (IR) in assuming data administration responsibilities.

Data Access. If knowledge is power, then the issue of data access (knowledge access) is perhaps the most important and politically sensitive element of data administration. Questions of who is allowed what access to which data bases at what point in time cut across all activities of an institution. The type and extent of problems engendered by the relatively simple question of data access are confounded by combining the desire for data with legal, data security, and data validity concerns.

Unfortunately, there are no correct answers to these questions. The policies, practices, and politics of an institution probably will dictate data access procedures. A system administrator (an administrator who has control of and responsibility for an official data base) might be reluctant to provide open access to data for fear they will be misunderstood and misused. System administrators tend to be extremely sensitive about data that have implications for institutional funding, accreditation, and program continuance. Users of the information may have to prove themselves to be responsible and capable of understanding the intricacies and anomalies of the data in order to gain and retain access. In contrast, a system administrator might view the expanded access as an opportunity to provide an increased level of data quality. Users who can see a direct link between the quality of information entered into a data base and the quality of the reports generated are more conscientious in reporting and auditing data.

Data Integrity. The concern about data integrity (data timeliness, accuracy, completeness, and consistency) is widespread. Frequent users of data, whether the data are generated by a computer or by other tabulation procedures, soon develop expectations concerning the data. Data are expected to be timely: Faculty expect rosters the first day of classes. Data are expected to be accurate: Funding agencies expect accurate counts of students, particularly if funding is related to enrollment. Data are expected to be complete: Summary information is expected at an appropriate level, for example, of departments or schools. Additionally, data are expected to be consistent: Enrollment at multicampus institutions reported by the individual campuses should agree.

When official institutional data bases are updated regularly, frequent users expect timely reports after the appropriate set of updates. Failure to update as expected often increases the demand by users for access to current data to meet their needs.

Finally, data integrity requires constant vigilance. It is important to test the reasonableness of the data regardless of whether the data are produced by routine or ad hoc procedures. The conscientious institutional researcher will scrutinize data routinely, and the importance of this habit needs to be conveyed to other users of the data.

Data Manipulation. If a data administration overview function does not formally exist, an institutional research office that is a primary user of the data is likely to be the de facto data administrator. Although administrative computing personnel usually are responsible for the operation, maintenance, and technical aspects of all administrative data bases, they are not often asked to analyze the data in the same way an institutional researcher would. The IR professional who analyzes data over time must be aware of cumulative artifactual changes in the data. To properly manipulate data, the questions to be answered include: Which departmental names have been changed? Which departments have merged with other departments and no longer exist? When did departments change schools? Have changes occurred in the course drop/add policy? When were standardized test scores (or other data fields) loaded into the data base?

While administrative computer programmers develop expertise in the particular system for which they are responsible, institutional researchers should develop a working knowledge of administrative data systems. Through work in several systems, institutional research personnel can become knowledgeable about many aspects (especially the contents) of the different systems. When data in certain fields are not reported or configured as expected, or other fields are not updated until a certain time, this information affects analysis. These bits and pieces of information about data should be collected and formally recorded for use by other users. Ideally, these data about data, or metadata, should be stored in a data element dictionary (DED). A well-documented DED is key to successfully decentralizing data.

Data Analysis and Interpretation. If data are made available in a machine-readable form to units outside administrative computing or the office of the system administrator, then a consulting function is needed to assure that the data are being properly analyzed and interpreted. While this function could be placed in any of several offices, the institutional research office with expertise in using and analyzing data resources can provide guidance about how to approach data base and related analytical problems.

Users who plan to do their own programming and analysis using fourth-generation, user-friendly programming tools are commonly referred to as end-users. First-time users of these tools should not necessarily be expected to generate accurate data when the answer requires looping through one or more segments of a hierarchical data base or omitting certain records based on derived fields. As the institutional research office consults with users of the data, they will discover what portions of the DED are not definitive and can then augment the DED accordingly.

Data Reporting. Interpretation of data requires an understanding of the procedures used to collect the data and the algorithms used to generate the report. Computer-generated reports require the same attention as manually prepared reports. Routine auditing of reports is necessary in order to uncover errors in data and logic.

Standard snapshots of administrative data bases that freeze computer records at key times facilitate the production and reporting of consistent results. For example, student records must be frozen routinely as of a census date for counting students. This permits various analyses of the data using the same population.

However, it is always distressing to users of computer-based data to discover that routine computer reports have been altered by hand, making it impossible to reconstruct these reports without assistance from the person who made the alterations. If standard enrollment reports are hand-adjusted by the registrar to reflect changes in the data before publication, it will be impossible to match subsequent computer analyses of the data with published counts. Such practices thwart users who attempt to tie their data analyses to official published reports, and these off-the-books adjustments constitute a problem that will become more serious as the number of end-users increases.

Data Administration in Institutional Research:
A Case Study of the University of Kansas, Lawrence

In the early 1970s, the University of Kansas, like many institutions of higher education, experienced tremendous demand from administrative offices for new centralized data systems, and for updating older systems. Even though there was a scarcity of computing personnel and limited resources to design new systems, the basic approach to meet this demand was to develop and implement systems as quickly as possible. In this environment, the analytical and qualitative dimensions of data were subordinate to the technical demands of data base administration and the quantitative demands of system administrators.

By the early 1980s, the combined impact of powerful and easy-to-use microcomputers, the trend toward decentralization of institutional data, and the growing demand for access to university information was forcing the university to focus on the integrity of data. System administrators and university officials realized that multiple, contradictory, and biased interpretations of the same central institutional data could seriously damage the external reputation and internal management of the university. In any data free-for-all, there would be no winners. It was clear that the establishment of a data administration function was essential. The only question was who would undertake that function. In 1985, the Office of Institutional Research and Planning (OIRP) at the University of Kansas, Lawrence (KU) was assigned responsibility for data administration. There are three principal reasons for that decision.

First, OIRP is a heavy user of university data for analytical and reporting purposes. For over a decade, OIRP computer programmers have extracted, reviewed, analyzed, and reported data from every major KU computer data base, and OIRP research staff have become very sensitive to the quality of data. Clearly, it is the office most familiar with the subtleties and shortcomings of the broad range of institutional data and data bases.

Second, the long-standing, extensive, and positive working relationships OIRP has established with offices throughout the university place it in a unique position to see the information needs and data uses of both university central administration and the decentralized academic departments and administrative units. From this perspective, institutional research can objectively assess and design the procedures and protocols required to implement effective data administration.

Third, the position of OIRP within the university administrative structure, that is, reporting to the University Director of Information Resources, and its professional staff, well qualified to undertake these responsibilities, makes it an ideal location for the data administration function.

After OIRP was formally assigned the responsibility for data administration, a staff member with extensive programming and analytical experience was designated as the data administrator (DA). A primary responsibility of the DA has been the development and maintenance of DEDs. The data administrator has developed machine-readable DEDs for the student records and human resources information systems. Upon approval, users may receive hard or machine-readable copies of the dictionaries. In addition to developing and maintaining DEDs, the data administrator has worked with users and representatives of the university information center to ensure that information requested by users is available.

In order to assure consistent policies and procedures relative to official university data bases, a Data Administration Committee was established. Members of the committee include information resources managers and executives, data system administrators, university information center representatives, and OIRP data administration staff. Working with this committee, the data administrator has developed and implemented policies to maintain the integrity of information downloaded from university mainframe computers to microcomputers, and to inform users of the legal and ethical responsibilities they assume when they receive such information.

Prior to gaining access to official university extract files, users must obtain written permission from the appropriate system administrator. In most cases, this permission is processed by the data administrator by describing on a standard form the user's data needs and intended use of the information. This form is sent to the system administrator for approval.

In 1985, the University of Kansas purchased a fourth-generation language package. As a result, users may access extracts from the student records, human resources, and financial systems. In addition to these systems, some users have defined their own operational files. For example, the Museum of Natural History has established an inventory of its collections.

The value-added aspect of institutional research involvement in this area is highlighted by the standing suggestion that users consult with OIRP data administration staff in order to gain a better understanding of the data they are requesting. Data administration staff have consulted with numerous units across campus on a variety of topics, including data base content (field names and values), schedules for updating data bases, and data access methodologies. Thus, data administration provides an increasingly vital service of helping users gather, manipulate, and interpret data. In a consultant role, the data administrator guides the user in applying proven and accepted algorithms and calculations. The data administrator explores efficient programming codes and makes suggestions for adapting existing codes appropriate to the nature of the information the user wants.

Finally, by manipulating available data and deriving new information, with the assistance of the data administrator, the user generates needed information and perhaps expands information contained in the DED as a by-product of the analysis. A data administrator who has command of both the mechanical and interpretive complexities of computing and data derivation will provide the most efficient and effective service to users.

The future plans for OIRP in data administration include:

- Increasing the information contained in existing DEDs and documenting additional systems
- Creating a Data Administration procedures manual
- Working with the Data Administration Committee to reduce paperwork

- Developing procedures for correcting errors in data and assuring data integrity
- Expanding and enhancing user consulting activities.

Summary

For OIRP, and perhaps any other institutional research offices actively involved in data operations, data administration has both problems and promise. The problems likely to be encountered by IR in data administration include:

- Data administration is time consuming, requires unfailing attention to detail, and consumes considerable human and financial resources.
- Extensive data management and coordination efforts are needed, especially during initial development and implementation of administrative protocols.
- Diligence must be exercised constantly in order to keep data administration a high priority in ongoing office responsibilities.
- The separation of data administration from data base administration may result in unlinked data element dictionaries, which would require even greater coordination efforts by IR.

The assignment of data administration to institutional research holds out these opportunities:

- Assisting in the development and design of universitywide data systems—a direct result of OIRP working closely with users and developing an understanding of user data needs.
- Separating the gatekeeper function (institutional research) from the owner (system administrator) provides users with a first line of appeal to institutional research if system administrators deny access to users.
- Helping users meet their information needs by drawing upon experience to know if requested information currently exists or if data will need to be extracted.
- Understanding users' information needs in order to configure data in new formats for broad-based distribution across campus.

An administrative function performed by a research operation is a challenge. Every effort must be made to balance the needs of the institution and the needs of various users to ensure that data and information are understood by users, and to see that the outcomes make sense. Because institutional research uses operational data bases extensively, it has a vested interest in maintaining the information flow from, access to, and the integrity of these data bases. Since institutional research strives for institutional information to be reported on a consistent basis, it is crucial that other departments accessing computer-based information be knowlegeable about data in order to accurately report them.

The role of institutional research in data administration is an evolutionary one with diverse and somewhat contradictory elements. While data integrity must be more closely monitored to ensure accuracy, it is appropriate that institutional research facilitate broad-based use of, and access to, data. This tight/loose contradiction can lead to administrative and management problems. While some users may require close monitoring to prevent data abuse, other less-experienced but interested users may need coaxing to take their first step into the water. In both cases, the demands on institutional research will be significant, but effort will be expended in different directions. Clearly, the role of institutional research in data administration is likely to be as political as it is managerial.

References

Barnett Data Systems. *Data Administration: Development and Practice.* Rockville, Md.: Barnett Data Systems, 1982a.

Barnett Data Systems. *Data Dictionaries: Concepts, Contents, and Uses.* Rockville, Md.: Barnett Data Systems, 1982b.

Hoffman, R.D.R. "Optical Disks: A Records-Management Bandage." *Information Week*, 1986, ... (83), p. 40.

Plourde, P. J. "Computing Trends and Strategies." *CAUSE/EFFECT*, 1986, *9* (3), 23–25.

Uhrbach, H. "The Systems Development Life Cycle (SDLC) in a Data Base/Data Dictionary Environment." In H. Uhrbach (ed.), The Data Dictionary in Systems Development. Lexington, Mass.: DBD Systems, 1980.

Richard L. McKinney is the data administrator and principal analyst with the Office of Institutional Research and Planning (OIRP) at the University of Kansas. The development of the data administration function at OIRP has been one of his primary responsibilities.

John S. Schott is assistant director of OIRP. His principal areas of responsibility are finance and budgeting.

Deborah J. Teeter is director of OIRP. She is active in the development of the data administration responsibilities for OIRP.

Linda W. Mannering is a principal analyst at OIRP. Her areas of responsibilities include microcomputing applications and the development of administrative support systems.

What will be the impact of technology and accountability on the distributed support of decision systems? What sources of influence are available for those who seek to provide such support in the new information age?

Decision Support in the Information Age

Gerald W. McLaughlin, Josetta S. McLaughlin, Richard D. Howard

Helping policy makers make better decisions is a crucial function in managing higher education. A major task in this function is ensuring that the decision maker has useable facts for making the decisions. The technological explosion of the information age and the shift to a more accountable management style have created a new and disruptive situation for those involved in providing and analyzing information to support decision making. The management information and analyses must be provided not only for central decision making but for decision makers throughout the institution. To provide effective support, products and processes of the management information and analysis function must be adapted to meet the varying needs of distributed decision makers. Consistent use of information requires that those in the management information and analysis function retain their influence. This is best done by those who understand the opportunities for influence inherent in the responsibilities of the data summarizing function. It is also useful to understand general strategies that can help maintain influence. The influence developed through these means is needed if policy and decision makers are to be helped rather than inundated by a sea of information. For example, a recent AT&T (1986)

E. M. Staman (ed.). *Managing Information in Higher Education.*
New Directions for Institutional Research, no. 55. San Francisco: Jossey-Bass, Summer 1987.

advertisement warned that "today as the Information Age has begun, there is new kind of isolation. People are awash in a mounting sea of information, unable to connect or work with information in an orderly, useful form."

When institutional research emerged as a profession, scientific decision making was just coming of age. Furniture-sized machines with 64K memory used machine language to move and manipulate data. Complicated code and switch-controlled consoles made computers the domain of a technical subculture. The cost of machines ensured that the subculture reported to the top of the organization, which in turn took a personal interest in the production and use of information. Those in the management information and analysis function (MIAF) were protected by those they served and insulated by the neo-mysticism of their craft.

Interest in the uses of information has retained its intensity over the years but the environment has changed. Information providers involved in the metamorphosis of decision making find themselves forced from their traditional relationships and power bases. Those processing information into one specific point in the organization must suddenly restructure the information development and transmitting functions to meet broader requirements for data at multiple levels of the organization. The infusion of high-tech computers, communications, and information systems has changed the world of information processing.

This change has particularly impacted personnel who function as management information and analysis specialists. For purposes of this chapter, the management information and analysis function is defined as an activity that involves working with facts at the information level, that is, developing useable facts from data. In addition it will involve working with facts at the knowledge level, that is, structuring the information so that it helps the decision maker in a specific situation. In today's institutions there tend to be three principal locations where MIAF is performed. The one familiar to many is the formal institutional research office. MIAF is a traditional function within institutional research that in many cases evolved out of the ability to write computer programs in support of external reporting. A second and newer organizational sub-unit evolving from the need to provide end-user support is the information center. The end-user wants to make decisions but may not be prepared to translate data for that purpose. The third location, which represents a return to the time before institutional research became prominent in higher education, is the specialized staff member. This individual may be attached to a specific office and have the title of "assistant to the . . . ," "associate . . . for administration," " . . . analyst," or some similar title.

The remainder of this chapter is intended to assist those who perform MIAF for the central administration regardless of their location within the organization. They must now face the new realities brought about by a changed environment. Emphasis is shifting from long-range planning to strategic management. No longer is it sufficient to use information simply to predict the future; consideration must also be given to the development of information in the present to influence the future. As a result, assessment of the proper role of MIAF is becoming increasingly difficult. MIAF is both a contributor to the increasing sea of information and the method by which the new kind of isolation can be remedied. This chapter is intended to help those in MIAF at colleges and universities to evaluate their role in influencing the development and transmission of information.

Technology Push and Market Pull

Increased availability of hardware, software, and operating systems has made information accessible to parts of colleges and universities other than central administration. Inexpensive, powerful and "user-friendly" computing resources are at everyone's fingertips. Instead of total dependence on large expensive mainframe computers with legions of personnel to manage and run them, small microcomputers that can interface with the mainframe or stand alone have become prominent in most offices. With increased use of this technology, computer literacy has increased across campus.

Advances in technology also allow downloading of institutional data bases to offices with intelligent devices. Information providers can make it possible for personnel throughout an organization to access large volumes of information for decision making. The technological capability is present but an important question has not yet been adequately addressed. Has an effective "distributed support system" for decision making been realized? Has the information provider developed policies and procedures for systematic training of personnel who are to be entrusted with the data? The ramifications of failing to develop adequate policies cannot be underestimated. According to Canning (1983), organizations distributing machine-readable data without adequate policy preparations have found: (1) their internal control systems weakened, (2) end-users reaching erroneous conclusions due to the failure of data to meet quality expectations, and (3) possible loss of data integrity in central files where the users have the ability to update information. Current concerns over the perplexing sea of information indicate that many in the MIAF may have failed to heed Canning's warning.

To design adequate policies for an effective information development and transmitting function requires an evaluation of the needs of all stakeholders, that is, all individuals who are directly affected by or involved in the process. Access to computer technology impacts stakeholders differently at various levels of the organization. It is therefore important to understand that the specific needs of the information user differ based on the decision style of the individual and the style dominant at each level of administration.

Table 1, adapted from work by Driver (1983) divides the administration of a university or college into five levels. With the exception of the cross-level category, each level is characterized by its own decision style, planning process, and information requirement. At the highest level of the administration, decision style is decisive, with information needs focusing on specific problems. Once the information is obtained and the decision made, focus shifts to implementation with generally no further need for information on the topic. By contrast, the decision style of senior faculty tends to be flexible, using just enough data to arrive at a solution. There is greater tendency to adapt or shift to another option whenever the environment changes. Among deans and department chairpersons, the requirement is for a continuous flow of information with strategic management needing the broad base required for continued responsiveness. Because the information needs vary across the different levels, MIAF must confront the resulting demand through development of both the technical ability to manipulate data at these different levels and the policies necessary for constructive use of information. Policies and procedures can no longer be tailored to reinforce a role solely at the top level of organizational structure.

Just as decision styles have been identified that define differing needs at various levels of the administration, different administrative styles have been identified across the various colleges and universities (Peterson,

Table 1. Decision Styles and Information Requirements as a Function of Organizational Level

Administrative Level	Decision Style	Planning Process	Information Requirement Breadth	Flow
President/VP	Decisive	Discrete	Focused	Discrete
Deans	Hierarchic	Long range linear	Focused	Continuous
Dept. chairmen	Integrative	Multiple options	Broad	Continuous
Senior faculty	Flexible	Adaptive	Broad	Discrete
Cross level				
Anywhere	Lurcher	Acceptance	None	None
Sponge	Avoidance	Unbounded	Eternal	
Systematic	Strategic Mgt.	Funneled	Restrictive	

Source: Adapted from Driver, 1983.

Table 2. Characteristics of Administrative Philosophies

| Characteristics | Administrative Philosophy | | |
	Collegial	Monarchy	Managerial
PLANNING			
Type	Cultural	Linear	Interpretive
Focus	Values	Goals	Opportunities
Values	Intrinsic	Extrinsic	Pragmatic
Needs	Social	Safety	Professional
Information	Gestalt	Forecast	Alternatives
ORGANIZING			
Type	Informal	Formal	Matrix
Operations	Decentralized	Centralized	Balanced
System	Amorphous	Closed	Open
DIRECTING			
Authority	Acceptance	Line/Staff	Functional
Behavior	Internalized	Coerced	Contracted
Response	Moral	Discipline	Rational
CONTROLLING			
Constraint	Purposes	Procedures	Policies
Concern	Processes	Production	Situational
Information	Spontaneous	Structural	Distributive
SUPPORTING INFORMATION NEEDS			
Activity	Technology	Operations	Training
Strategy	Reactive	Linear	Interpretive
Leverage	Goodwill	Power	Influence
Requirement	Decentralized	Restricted	Coordinated

1985; Chaffee, 1985). These administrative styles, like decision style, affect the market for information by changing the way information is injected into the organization. Table 2 gives insight into the type of environment in which the MIAF might be performed. It should be noted that changing administrative styles lead to changes in organizational roles and culture. For those in the MIAF, these changes focus on supporting information needs. This support differs across the three styles considered.

Three major styles of administration are apparent in higher education: collegial, monarchical and managerial. It is useful to consider the procedures for transmitting information under each of these styles. In the collegial style, information transmission can be both developed and infused into the decentralized groups of senior faculty. There is little need to coordinate the numbers since data are not exported and often not put into conflict. Decisions are frequently made based on qualitative concerns. Information needs of users under the collegial style require a highly technical decentralized support system capable of responding to broad requirements.

In the monarchical style, the information flow is channeled into the top level of the organization. A centralized support system supports centralized decision making. A consistent set of numbers is important and achievable since there is only one set of numbers. Information needs under the monarchical style appear best served by efficient operations that focus on a restricted flow of information into the top levels of the organization.

The managerial style pushes decisions to the operations level where flexibility and knowledge support a multitude of decisions intended to influence the future. Unlike the first case, decisions are reached based on quantitative concerns. Information must be transmitted to all levels of the organization. Decentralized decision making, which requires control and coordination of numbers, requires a distributed support system, that is, one providing coordinated support at all levels of the organization. MIAF must therefore consider training others to use the data correctly. Information flow needs to be coordinated. Influence through shaping perceptions of decision makers replaces the formal mandates of power conferred by the monarch.

The changing environment has moved institutions of higher education closer to the managerial style. Technology push has moved the locus of activity down the organization while market pull arising out of newly defined needs at lower levels of the organization has resulted in new demands being placed on providers of information. As noted earlier, those in MIAF have been drawn away from the traditional power bases. New, perhaps more interpretive, strategies must now be adopted. Consideration must be given to a more productive approach to influence, that is, use of tactics that increase credibility in ways that benefit both those in MIAF as well as the organization.

Information demands of different groups of decision makers and the need to coordinate quantitative information requires that those in MIAF be in a position to shape the development and use of information. The shift to the managerial style and the relative loss of technical expertise removes the traditional method that those in MIAF used to challenge the sea of information.

A New Awareness for Those in MIAF

A more proactive approach by those in MIAF is consistent with the managerial style. If the information age has created uncertainty about the traditional role of MIAF in influencing the appropriate use of facts, understanding the process of producing useable knowledge and information from facts is basic to reinstating structure into the environment.

Specialists in MIAF begin with a body or group of facts, typically a data base, and create useable knowledge by structuring and focusing information to meet the needs of the decision maker. Opportunities arise for MIAF as a result of this close proximity to the body of facts and expertise in working with these data. Opportunities also arise when MIAF works closely with decision makers in the institution. These opportunities for influence inherent in the function of informational support of decision makers can be grouped into five-categories.

Access. Data are the raw materials of any MIAF. While the capture and storage of data are traditionally not a concern, MIAF access to the data bases, the computers where the data are stored, and the software to transform the facts is important if MIAF is to meet the needs of decision makers. Satisfied decision makers are influential. Access to decision makers is equally important. Otherwise, there is less opportunity to focus MIAF on important problems.

Information Development. Information development requires involvement in establishing procedures for ensuring the quality of the data. If the data are secure, accurate, and stable, MIAF will have more credibility in its interaction with users. Additional value can be added to the function through development of timely and relevant information reports at an acceptable cost.

Knowledge Development. Knowledge development rests on the skill and ability of those in MIAF to seize opportunities as a result of their knowledge of characteristics of the data and software. This enables them to transform data from their raw state to their knowledge state. This is enhanced by knowledge of the decision process itself. If the process is still in the definition phase, facts should be brought to bear that help define the situation prior to making the decision. Superfluous facts disrupt the process. Also important in knowledge development within the institution is the vertical integration of MIAF with data base administration and telecommunications to reduce the potential for disruptive influences in the flow of facts. MIAF can thus position itself to perform a critical role in preventing different information activities from supporting incompatible goals.

User Support. By developing prototype decision support, those in MIAF can demonstrate the potential value of their function. User support also involves anticipating needs and situations, establishing links with key elements in the institutional decision process, and helping decision makers use facts more effectively. In many cases this will involve education of decision makers on things from the availability of various facts through learning how to model hypothetical situations. User support will be more effective when both MIAF and the user understand who is responsible for what types of information and analysis. Some users will just want the facts. Others prefer the analysis with recommendations.

Distribution. Distribution opportunities are the category most directly affected by the new information age. The MIAF support system must now serve many points in the organization simultaneously. In the past, this function occurred only in a central location, if at all. This necessitates teaching personnel at all levels of the organization about MIAF. Some of this teaching may involve how to use computers and software while some training may involve how to perform basic institutional research functions. MIAF may want to establish user groups to reinforce this training.

In the final analysis, MIAF must take advantage of opportunities to become a focal point for information development and processing. It should be equipped to access information, manipulate data, and exercise quality control over the distributed support system. The role of MIAF in defining its value to the institution should be carefully incorporated into the strategic planning process and reinforced with the appropriate policies.

Strategies less dependent on policies and focusing on changing the perception of MIAF can also be useful for influencing the distributed support of decision systems. The following vehicles of attitude change are less related to the information production process, but they can be sources of influence for those in MIAF.

Communication. Focus on increased communication with other units. Formal and informal networks can be used to develop committees that identify issues concerning the need for and uses of information. An outreach function can be developed that asks stakeholders "What can I do to help you today?" Effective communication also includes a sense of timing that will produce the needed information at the proper time and in the proper form.

Credibility. Those in MIAF must be seen as credible. Credibility initially stemmed from members of the top administration viewing those in MIAF as technically competent professionals. MIAF personnel must now be seen by members at all levels of the distributed system as doing quality work in a timely fashion. They must also be seen as having integrity, honesty, and discretion. Helping to resolve questions of data security is beneficial. The ability to help ensure consistent numbers and clearly understand data element definitions will also go a long way to establishing credibility.

Coordination. Provide constructive communication between units of the organization. This can be especially important as the process moves to distributed information. In the past, weak documentation of data bases has often produced inconsistent numbers when new users started to use institutional data. This can be best resolved by linking the needs of users with the "mysteries" of the data, a function that those in MIAF must be ready to perform.

Development of user-friendly institutional data bases can make internal information generally available to operating units other than those who captured the data. In addition, those in MIAF have information concerning decision style and issues internal and external to the organization that affect all stakeholders in the distributed support system.

Commitment. Commitment by decision makers is made both to principles and to individuals. Those in MIAF can direct the use of information in a manner that strengthens the organization's ability to meet these commitments and to accomplish its goals. Some strategies might include developing position papers that identify and strengthen common institutional commitments. "The Role of Effective Undergraduate Education," "The Contribution of Research to the State," or "Economic Impact of Alumni" are examples of titles that might describe efforts to uphold the commitment to principles. By contrast, the commitment to individuals requires building alliances with key stakeholders in various units.

Leveraging. Use power bases built through technical skills to develop effective working relations and to influence third parties. For example, if a dean is responsive to free technical support, he can be a source of influence with other deans. If department chairpersons are appreciative of committee work focusing on a key concern, they can be a source of influence with their dean. The intention is not to suggest that those in MIAF become master politicians but it is important for them to do environmental scanning and consider the human side of the enterprise.

Authority. For those in MIAF, authority has traditionally been based on a centralized rather than a distributed support system. While the formal authority of the monarch may no longer be available, the functional authority attained through the traditional role can be used to assist the stakeholders in the new distributed support system in meeting their goals and ultimately the goals of the institution itself. In this endeavor, it seems appropriate for those in MIAF to concern themselves with teaching others how to use information. In many cases the success of a decision-support effort comes only after the decision maker is talked through the decision and the information is structured into a form that focuses on essential elements of information and the uncertainty in the decision. This is a complex process requiring skill that is different from the ability to use software for the production of numbers.

Conclusions

The preceding discussion has sought to chart some alternatives for those in MIAF under changing conditions. Different decision and administrative styles pull our resources in different directions and create challenges that did not exist in the past. If the forces are as presented, then the challenges must be faced. There is no return to the past.

The basis of this chapter is the belief that those in MIAF have the professional knowledge, skills, and abilities to focus information on the needs of decision makers in our colleges and universities, and in the sense that the goals and values of those in MIAF are consistent with the broader needs of higher education. Strategies were sought that will allow those in MIAF to retain the ability to influence the use of information within their institution. The solution is to distribute coordinated support to decision makers. The confusion that will result from failing to take this approach is evident.

MIAF personnel may never have been more important than now, as they fulfill the role of providing coordinated distributed support of decision systems. At the same time, those in MIAF must look beyond this one objective. Their goal must be to develop a sense of what the future holds for MIAF, on the assumption that this future can be constructively influenced. Those in MIAF who best understand their environment with its challenges and opportunities, who best understand their function with its strengths and weaknesses, and who best understand the strategic characteristics in the process of producing information, will be best prepared to influence the future.

References

AT&T. "Promises Kept: Promises to Keep." *Washington Monthly,* Nov. 1986, p. 5.

Canning, R. G. "Controlling Distributed Data." *EDP Analyzer,* 1983, *21* (9).

Chaffee, E. E. "The Concept of Strategy: From Business to Higher Education." In J. C. Smart (ed.), *Higher Education: Handbook of Theory and Research.* New York: Agathon Press, 1985.

Driver, M. "Decision Style and Organizational Behaviors: Implications for Academia." *The Review of Higher Education,* 1983, *6* (4), 387–406.

Peterson, M. W. "Emerging Developments in Post-Secondary Organization Theory and Research: Fragmentation or Integration?" *Educational Research,* 1985, *14* (3), 5–12.

Gerald W. McLaughlin is associate director of Institutional Research and Planning Analysis at Virginia Polytechnic Institute and State University. His current interests include distributed institutional research functions as they support decision making and the use of analytical methodology. He is active in AIR and CAUSE.

Josetta S. McLaughlin is a doctoral candidate and graduate assistant in Business Policy at Virginia Polytechnic Institute and State University. She holds a master's degree in Consumer Studies and is active in several consumer associations. Her interests include strategic management and organizational policy analysis.

Richard D. Howard is currently director of Institutional Research at North Carolina State University. Formerly he was director of Institutional Research at West Virginia University. His current interests include planning and decision support as related to university data bases. He is active is AIR, CAUSE, and SCUP.

*Computing and information processing have evolved to a
point where colleges and universities have both a need and
a well-timed opportunity to develop guidelines and policy
statements for the management and control of data.*

Policies and Practices
for Ensuring Data Integrity

E. Michael Staman

New Environments

As the use of computing in support of administrative functions in
colleges and universities has grown, approaches to handling, storing, and
retrieving data have changed dramatically. From manually written and
stored records, colleges and universities have moved to magnetically
encoded records on disk and tape. These records, originally stored as single-use files, have become large, integrated data bases with multiple uses.
Access to these data bases is changing from printed reports to on line
inquiries, and centrally controlled batch updating is being replaced by
data entered via a terminal by a user in his or her own office. The use of
microcomputers for data access and analysis is becoming common. Thus,
the methodologies of data maintenance and usage are evolving rapidly.

Apart from the mechanisms of data storage and retrieval, however,
the larger issues of management and control of data exist, issues that normally require policy statements and guidelines from upper management.
The purpose of this chapter is to recommend models for policies and
procedures that address the areas of data ownership, confidentiality, privacy, and security. Most college and university data centers should be able
to adopt the recommendations, rewriting and tailoring them to their specific environments.

E. M. Staman (ed.). *Managing Information in Higher Education.*
New Directions for Institutional Research, no. 55. San Francisco: Jossey-Bass, Summer 1987.

Ownership

The ownership of all data bases clearly resides with the institution. However, the institution should designate responsibility to a steward for each of its data sets. The institution itself should not be the steward.

Traditionally, the stewardship function has rested with the computing organization. In an institution with a relatively small set of applications accessing dedicated or single-use data sets containing only basic data, this approach functions adequately. Over time, however, in many institutions these systems have evolved and matured to the point where they require data that can only be supplied by systems that are maintained and monitored by other administrative areas. Furthermore, the data contained within these systems have been expanded from a very limited set to a comprehensive resource, and now require a new generation of data support methods, procedures, and policies.

In effect, the key skill or knowledge in the old environment was related to computing hardware or software; in the new environment, it is knowledge about data and its use. There has been an orientation away from mechanical skills and toward service and applications.

Suggested Environment. Based on these background consideration, the data sets in this environment need a designated steward, preferably from within a user department or division, for example, the comptroller might be the steward of financial information data sets. In the suggested environment, every data base and subset of a data base has a designated steward responsible for the integrity and content of the data. In this context, integrity is defined as a measure of the quality, security, and confidentiality of the data within the data base, including extracts from the files. Content deals with the definition and description of data elements within a data base.

A data base is defined as any collection of records stored on a computer disk, tape, or other medium, or any extraction or subset of that collection of records including terminal display of data, printed reports, and data processing cards. A vital data base is a permanent set of data whose loss, destruction, alteration, or dissemination would severely harm the operational capability of the institution.

Model Recommendations. Create a policy relating to data bases that includes the designation of an appropriate steward for data bases currently existing or under development, the appointment of the steward by senior-level management from persons within the operating organization, and the assignment to the steward of responsibility for the integrity and content of the assigned data base. Also assign specific areas of responsibility to the steward, including

1. *Administration within the context of institutional policies and procedures.* The steward should have responsibility of decisions regarding

the data base. Where a decision affects several areas, the steward should be responsible for ensuring that the decision is made known at the appropriate levels.

2. *Definition of data elements.* The steward should be responsible for defining and describing data elements within the data base and for ensuring that these data elements meet the requirements of the institution. The institution's computer center should play an active role in this process. In addition, where an action may affect the operation of other segments of institutional administration, such groups should also be involved.

3. *Security, privacy, and confidentiality.* The steward should be responsible for ensuring that policies and procedures relating to security, privacy, and confidentiality of the data base are adequate and enforced.

4. *Funding.* The steward should be responsible for ensuring that a cost/benefit study is completed prior to development of a data base. This study should normally address funding and costs of the data base including development, maintenance, and storage. All such studies should have the active participation of the computer center.

5. *Training.* In order to provide the stewards with the specialized knowledge needed to perform their roles, the computer center should develop and administer a training program.

Confidentiality

A college or university has an interesting problem when dealing with confidentiality of data. If the institution is public, a portion of its data bases may already be or will become public records. It also collects and processes data that require a very high level of confidentiality. Therefore, the institution often must provide access to certain sets of data as requested, while strictly limiting access to other sets. Additionally, while some information may be public, it is the best interest of the institution to control the access to this information as well as the context in which the information is accessed and used.

Most institutions have developed and implemented security systems to protect data or programs from accidental or intentional destruction, and to prevent improper or unauthorized use of its computing resources. In a computing environment where the processing systems have been oriented toward producing hard-copy reports from single-use data bases, this security system has served the additional functions of limiting access and of providing some confidentiality of data. However, as colleges and universities begin implementing systems oriented toward access to integrated or multiple-use data bases, the use of a security system as a confidentiality or access system creates problems. The problems become evident when the objectives of a security and confidentiality system are examined.

The primary objective of a security system is to protect the data. This involves creating defenses that strictly limit access to the data resource. The role of a confidentiality system is to use the controls provided by the security system to allow structured and monitored access for purposes of update retrieval, while at the same time ensuring that the integrity of the data is maintained.

With respect to confidentiality, cause for concern in many environments is a high dependence on printed reports or hard copy. One of the most important keys to confidentiality is the limitation of the number of copies of a data element. In other words, the confidentiality of data is dependent on the number of persons who can gain access to it. Information on paper has a large potential audience. Thus, the greater the shift away from printed reports toward the use of terminal access, the greater the potential gain in the level of confidentiality.

There is a practical limit on the data for which one can reasonably expect to control access. While access to centrally developed data bases should be controlled, it is not practical to develop an access control system that addresses every possible data base developed by every organization within the institution. The confidentiality recommendations provided below are directed toward centrally developed data bases, but they could be used for any data base that shares the characteristics of the centrally developed ones.

Finally, it is important to note that all efforts to increase the confidentiality of a system will be limited by two major considerations. The first involves the requirements of external agencies and groups who both set access guidelines and require access for their own purposes. The second is the need to minimize the bureaucratic burden of implementing a set of policies and procedures.

Suggested Environments. Extreme care needs to be taken in developing a confidentiality system to prevent the imposition of cumbersome controls. A confidentiality system, like a security system, can be as complex and expensive as an institution desires. The prime objective, however, is to allow authorized persons easy access to data at a reasonable cost. The optimal solution is to provide centralized access control via stewards who are responsible for discrete, yet comprehensive, segments of a data resource.

Model Recommendations. Prepare a policy on confidentiality of data sets that includes:

- A comprehensive review of all data bases and subsets of data bases (what they contain, where they are, and so on) owned by the institution
- The establishment of a level of confidentiality for each data base and subset
- A review conducted by the designated data base steward that involves the internal auditing department, the computer center,

the legal department, and any users of the data beyond the office responsible for the data

- Three levels of confidentiality; available to anyone, available only to persons designated by the steward, and available only to the steward.

Charge the computer center with the following responsibilities:

- Conducting a systems-definition effort to define the specifications for a confidentiality/access control system that is implementable within the long-range computing strategies and philosophies of the institution
- Ensuring that the system specified permits easy access to data while allowing for the strict limitation of the data accessed
- Developing a confidentiality standards document to be followed by development efforts
- Encouraging and supporting, where possible, the use of non-hard copy access to data. Consideration should be given to developing a long-range program for substantially reducing the number of printed reports and restricting the data printed on existing reports to essential elements.

Privacy

Privacy is concerned with the rights of those individuals on whom data is maintained. In the broadest definition, an individual is a student, former student, alumnus, employee, contributor, or other person who interacts with or receives services from the institution.

As integrated data bases are developed and implemented, particularly within administrative areas, the potential for violation of an individual's privacy is increased. The problem is not unique to higher education. In addition to current legislation, general public concern has initiated legislative studies at the federal and state levels with the objectives of determining the need for legislation relating to the right to privacy with respect to data collection, maintenance, and dissemination.

It would appear that an institution should be able to assure any individual that it is not collecting excessive information about him or her, using it in unfair ways, or disseminating it indiscriminately. While it is impractical to review and receive concurrence from every individual on every element of data collected, processed, or disseminated, there should be an overall policy on privacy.

The following section recommends models for ensuring that the individual's rights to privacy are protected. Recognizing the impracticalities delineated earlier, it defines approaches that permit the assurance to individuals that their institution is aware of, and making conscientious efforts to ensure, individuals' rights to privacy.

The privacy of the individual is affected by several forces:

- The cost of capturing, processing, and storing data is continuing to decrease dramatically
- The implementation of data bases that are accessible by multiple applications systems is increasing rapidly
- The means to access data, either through terminals or in a printed form, are becoming more available and are easier to implement
- The increased awareness among the general public about the power and capability of computing systems, is resulting in an increased demand for data and analysis at all levels of institutions.

Institutions have the ability, in hardware, software, and development skill, to gather and organize significant amounts of data pertaining to any single individual, and, while there may be no intent to misuse this capability, it is possible that an institution might accidentally violate an individual's privacy or give the appearance of doing so.

Suggested Environment. In the suggested environment, two functions are addressed: the gathering of data and the release of information. Additionally, two types of data bases are concerned. The first is the formal, computer-supported data base developed by a central computing organization within a central administration or a campus. The second is developed by a department or individual and may or may not be computer-supported. These are discussed as formal and informal data bases, respectively.

Gathering Information. The key to privacy of data is control of the data gathering and dissemination processes, with emphasis on collecting only the data required. For formal data bases, the approach is to require that each data base being developed undergoes a privacy review. This review determines if there is a legitimate business requirement for each element of data within the data base. Over some reasonable period of time, reviews of currently existing data bases are conducted to assure that the same requirement is met. If not, corrective action is initiated to remove those data elements for which there is not a legitimate business need.

While the above review procedure is practical for formal data bases, it is impractical for informal data bases because of their number, size, and location. One possible alternative for these informal data bases is to exhibit good intentions and faith by developing and distributing management directives and bulletins that emphasize the need for institutional management to guard against collecting unauthorized data that could be used to violate an individual's privacy. Another alternative could be charging an internal auditing department with the function of evaluating the privacy standards of data bases and files identified in their normal auditing functions.

Release of Information. While the above procedures help to ensure privacy by limiting the data gathered, the release of data must also be addressed. In the suggested environment, management bulletins emphasizing the need for privacy and defining the types of information that can be released are distributed. At regular intervals the bulletins are reviewed for applicability and for agreement with other policies and directives, both internal and external.

Model Recommendations. Approve a policy stating that the institution is committed to protecting the privacy of an individual's records and that designated data base stewards will conduct privacy reviews on the information stored within the data bases to ensure that each piece of information related to an individual is required, that it is assigned the appropriate level of confidentiality, that safeguards are in place to prevent release of information in violation of policy, and to make certain that all reasonable efforts are taken to ensure the validity and reliability of all data. The reviews should include representatives from an internal auditing department, computing systems development, the legal office, and senior administration.

Also, charge the stewards with developing and issuing guidelines, on a regular basis, on the use of information contained in data bases under their control that relates to privacy of individuals and conduct a survey to identify potentially sensitive data bases that may have been developed, either formally or informally. Any such existing data bases should be brought into conformance with policy and procedures.

Security

The definition of security as it applies to data is relatively simple. It is the protection of data from accidental or intentional alteration or destruction. This definition can also include granting access to data only to authorized individuals. In other words, a piece of information placed in a secure computer-resident data base is retrievable by authorized individuals at any time, and that piece of information is unchanged in any way.

While the definition is relatively simple, the execution is not. The potential for security violation is virtually unlimited. A partial list includes floods and tornadoes, sabotage and fire, malfunction of hardware or software, and human error.

The number of ways that data can be destroyed is frightening. But in the end, all security systems must eventually depend upon an individual or group of individuals who have the knowledge and ability to break the security system. In effect, despite all the elaborate safeguards that may be developed, security will hinge on the integrity of an individual.

While the task of data security appears formidable, an institution must have a security program to protect vital data. Because it is not financially feasible or practical to address all possible exposures, it may be that the best possible plan is to limit the negative impact of a violation and to have a means of recovery in the least possible time. Concern for the safety of data should result in the selection of security measures that reduce the risk associated with storing the data within tolerable limits at the lowest cost.

Suggested Environment. Three areas are important in describing the suggested environment: the institution, computer facilities, and the steward or data base administrator.

The Institution. The institution has two major responsibilities. The first is that of providing direction and support for security. Like other functional areas, general management is responsible for setting policy and establishing goals. Once enunciated, it becomes the responsibility of other functional groups to conform to the stated policy and goals. The second responsibility of the institution is to set up a security group that continually reviews existing security policy to ensure that the desired level of security is being achieved. In addition, the security group reviews new laws and reporting requirements to determine if existing policy and procedures need revision to conform the changing environment. Finally, the group provides overall support for security throughout the institution.

In general, it seems appropriate to have an independent group whose responsibility is to oversee security throughout the institution. This group uses whatever expertise is required to certify that the policies concerning security are being followed and to help strengthen identified shortcomings. In the area of computer security, it is best that this group not be under the administrative control of any existing computer-management body.

Computer Facilities. It is the responsibility of a computer facility to provide security for all data located at the site. With much of an institution's data stored on computing systems, ongoing revisions need to be made to ensure that the data are protected against accidental and intentional destruction or modification.

Physical security includes policies and procedures for limiting access to the facility and limiting the introduction and removal of equipment (for example, computer equipment) and media (for example, paper, cards, tape volumes). In the event of a disaster (natural or otherwise), an in-place recovery plan will return the facility to operational status as quickly as possible. The plan is audited on a regular basis and modified as conditions warrant.

The institution's computer center provides hardware and software to ensure the integrity of the data resident at the site. In addition, the center provides reports or monitoring facilities to ensure the proper functioning of the security provisions. As new systems, hardware, or software are installed, verification of the security provisions is made to determine the impact of the new facilities.

In addition to providing for the safety of the data and hardware housed at the central site, the computer center also has responsibility for providing the remote sites with assistance or notification in the event that security provisions are threatened or have been breached. However, the integrity of data sent from remote sites is the responsibility of the remote site. Limiting access to the physical facilities is one safeguard for that integrity. For example, students studying operating systems should not be manipulating the same computer that is used to send grades to the central site. Another safeguard is releasing materials only to authorized representatives of the steward, and protecting the materials until such release.

The Steward or Data Base Administrator. Data base administration is an organizational role often created when traditional department bound aries are crossed. The thrust of computer data bases is to integrate operational data from diverse organizational units to facilitate management reporting. One side effect is to blur the identity of the single steward. A data base administrator should be the individual designated as the steward for the integrated data bases.

Stewardship responsibilities for physical facilities are limited to the equipment, usually terminals, under the steward's authority. The responsibilities for data integrity include:

- Input controls to validate data being placed in the computer system
- Back-up copies of data stored in the computer to protect against operational errors
- Off-site back-up copies to protect against natural disasters or other destructions surrounding the computer itself
- Audit trails to log activity with the data
- Procedural measures to prevent a single individual from controlling both the data entering and results exiting from the system
- Processing checks, including reasonableness checks, check digits, batch totals, record counts, and identification cross checks to ensure that data going into the computer are as valid as a machine can verify.

Data integrity safeguards should be tailored in accordance with a risk analysis conducted by the data base administrator or steward.

Access to the data is the responsibility of the steward. This responsibility includes the safeguarding and periodic changing of passwords. It includes proper safeguarding of the operating procedures used in the system to change data. It also includes establishing a procedure to authorize people to obtain or accept output. The intent is to prevent unauthorized individuals from obtaining computer output. Where access privileges are tied to a terminal under the steward's authority, access to the physical terminal must be limited. In short, the steward retains responsibilities for the data and processing results. Whether using manual methods or machine methods, responsibility for the end results remains with the steward.

The data base administrator or steward carries responsibility for communicating security awareness to institutional personnel and performing operational audits to ensure continued security. The role of the data base administrator also includes responsibility for the security of shared data or terminals. Where the steward role is divided, the responsibility for security is placed in the the data base administration role.

Security awareness begins with a risk analysis conducted on new computer uses. The risk analysis will determine the extent and nature of the security measures warranted for a system. Communicating security awareness acquaints people using the new system with the responsibilities of stewardship. The steward takes appropriate measures to meet the risks identified in the risk analysis. The role of data base administration is to maintain a complete list of alternative measures. Once these are initiated, data base administration is then responsible for periodic operational audits to ensure continued use of the security measures.

Model Recommendations. Approve a policy on data set security stating that all data sets designated as vital to the operation of the institution will be copied periodically and stored in a highly secure area located away from the computing facility holding the data set, and that this secure area will be sufficiently protected to ensure against destruction or theft of the data set by any reasonable force.

Charge the computer center with determining responsibility for data base security and whether current security systems need revising or upgrading.

Using the recommendations contained in the proposed environment section, develop a security manual. Based on this manual, conduct a set of security seminars on a continuing basis for data base administrators and stewards. The seminars should be designed to teach the use of the security system, define security responsibilities, and define effective procedures for security.

At a facilities level, establish a physical security task force that will understand back-up/recovery techniques and physical security; develop a physical security plan, including back-up and recovery procedure, for each major computing installation; and conduct annual reviews to identify additional measures or changes to the plan.

Summary

Computing and information processing have evolved to a point where many colleges and universities are presented with both the need and the opportunity to review and revise their policies on ownership, confidentiality, security, and privacy of institutional data. This chapter provided definitions and discussions of these policy issues, described a suggested environment for each, and offered a set of model recommendations that can be adapted by most institutions in creating institutional policies in these four areas.

E. Michael Staman has been involved in higher education since 1966, serving as a faculty member and in various administrative capacities in computing, institutional research, and planning.

Index

A

Academic computing: and academic departmental research, 31-34, 36-40, 45, 87; and computer-assisted instruction (CAI), 31-33, 37-39, 45; in distributed locations, 2, 35, 37, 40, 47; and a higher education institute, 38-40; history of, 29-32; and institutional research, 45, 71-80

Administration styles, 85-86

Administrative computing. *See* Management information and analysis functions (MIAF)

Administrator/Manager roles and responsibilities, 1, 8, 82, 89-90; of a chief information officer (CIO), 5-6, 10-11, 13, 17, 21, 25, 50, 77; of consultants, 10-11, 17, 24, 49-50, 53-55; of data administrators, 71-80; of data base stewards, 94-97, 99, 101-102; of departmental information officers, 25-26; in a higher education institute, 38-40; of an information center director, 23; of a manager of information systems (MIS), 16, 20, 22-24, 26, 50-51; of oversight groups, 4, 23, 25, 38-40, 53, 55-56, 78, 99-100; philosophies and decision styles of, 84-86; of a telecommunications manager, 50-56. *See also* Management information and analysis function (MIAF)

American Telephone and Telegraph Company (AT&T), 81, 90

B

Barnett Data Systems, 73, 80

Bentley College, 45

Bok, D., 29

Buildings ("smart") and energy management, 46-48. *See also* Telecommunications management

C

Canning, R. G., 83, 90

Case studies. *See* Model

Centrex (telephone exchange system), 49, 54

Chaffee, E. E., 85, 90

Communications. *See* Local area networks issues; Telecommunications

Community and vocational institutions, 45-46

Computer literacy and competency, 10, 20, 25, 35, 45, 49, 60, 83; and data use training, 9-10, 102; personal computers and, 34; self-instruction and, 33-35, 45, 62-68; and user support training, 9, 12, 16, 20-21, 26, 61-63, 79, 86-89, 98-99, 102

Computer science and computer-assisted instruction. *See* Academic Computing

Computerization, 6, 16; and data decentralization trends, 1, 5, 13, 15, 31, 45, 71-76, 82, 86, 93-95, 98; and declining automation costs, 8, 10, 34-36; and declining enrollment, 46; and demystification trends, 30-31, 82; and distributed functions trends, 1, 5, 7, 15, 31, 45; and equipment miniaturization, 29-30, 34, 72; and shared data base trends, 11-13, 48-49, 51-53, 55-56; and systems integration trends, 11-13, 51-53; and technological convergence, 15, 21; and technological proliferation, 49-51, 76-77; and user diversification trends, 60-61, 72. *See also* Systems management; Telecommunications

Creutz, A., 3, 57

D

Data administration, (analytical), 4, 7-8, 71-73; and access procedures, 21, 74, 87; and backlog problems, 10,

Office applications management *(continued)*
staff needs, 15, 18, 24; of writing and wordprocessing, 2, 18, 21-22, 32

P

Peterson, M. W., 84, 90
Phone input systems. *See* Telecommunications
Pittsburgh, University of, 45-46
Plourde, P. J., 72, 74, 80
Policies: decision style influences on, 84-86; information management planning and, 14, 23-26, 53-56. *See also* Systems management
Privacy and security issues, 95-103; forces affecting, 98
Programming. *See* Data base administration (technical); Software management
Programs. *See* Data bases; Fourth-generation languages

R

Research. *See* Applications management; Management information and analysis functions (MIAF)

S

Schott, J. S., 3, 67, 68, 71, 80
Security and public safety applications, 64-66, 95-96
Self-instruction, computerized. *See* Academic computing; Computer literacy and competency
Shakespeare, W., 37
Software management, 35-36, 39, 60, 67-68; of ad hoc programming and reports, 10-12, 61-62, 65, 75; and the computing services industry, 10-11; and development processes, 7-9, 22, 31, 39, 63-67; in-house and contracted, 10-11, 17, 24, 49-50, 55; and programming personnel, 59-60; at Western Michigan University, 63-67. *See* also Fourth-generation languages
Staman, E. M., 2, 4, 13, 61, 68, 93, 103
Student computing: and access issues, 101; information centers and labs for, 5, 9-10, 17, 23, 25-26, 31-32, 34; and required personal computers, 45-46; user group needs, 20, 33, 35, 37, 45, 56. *See also* Academic computing
Students and computerization: of activity records, 31, 33, 44, 72, 75-76; of admissions, recruitment, and retention, 3, 8, 11, 45-47, 62; of enrollment, 75-76; privacy rights of, 97; of registration and class scheduling, 7, 44, 51; of testing and scoring, 31, 33, 44, 62, 75, 101
Subject areas, computerized. *See* Academic computing; Data base administration
Systems management, (distributed), 2, 5-8, 15, 35, 37, 43, 47; environments and configurations, 39-40, 44, 48-49, 56; financial implications of, 34, 37; and MIAF, 88; policies, 43. *See also* Local area networks issues
Systems management, (integrated), 2, 6, 23, 25, 36, 38-40, 53-56, 65-66, 68; policy models, 93-103; and shared data bases, 3, 11-13, 48- 49, 51-53, 55-56. *See also* Environments and configurations

T

Teeter, D. J., 3, 67, 68, 71, 80
Telecommunications management, 2, 16, 25; of applications, 3, 33, 35, 45-46, 48-56, 82; business-style planning of, 53-56; centralized and distributed, 3, 51-53; and electronic mail, 19, 51; equipment technology and, 46-49; and local area networks, 15, 22, 35, 39-40, 44, 48-49; and MIAF, 87-88; and telephone systems, 43-44, 47, 51
Temple University, 46
Toynbee, A., 30
Training in data administration, 62-67, 86, 95, 102. *See also* Computer literacy and competency

U

Uhrbach, H., 73, 80
User group roles and needs, 12, 17, 19, 22-24, 74; of academic departments

and faculty, 1, 36-40, 47, 56, 84, 86; of administrators, 1, 8; convergence of, 21, 25, 53, 60, 63, 67, 72; diversity of, 60-61, 72; of external agencies, 75, 95-97; of information specialists, 3, 61-65; of institutional researchers, 71-72, 74-76, 76-80; of office staffs (knowledge workers), 15, 18, 24. *See also* Administrator/Manager roles and responsibilities; Student computing

V

Vertical integration. *See* Management information and analysis (MIAF); Systems management
Virginia Polytechnic Institute, 45

W

Warren, S., 2-3, 29, 41
Western Michigan University, 63-67
White, T. H., 36